THE CTS COLLECTION

THE CTS COLLECTION

TRAINING TIPS FOR CYCLISTS AND TRIATHLETES

Carmichael Training Systems

FEATURING **Chris Carmichael**

FOREWORD BY **Lance Armstrong**

EDITED BY **Jim Rutberg**

VELO *press*®

Boulder
Colorado

The CTS Collection: Training Tips for Cyclists and Triathletes
© 2001 Carmichael Training Systems

Printed in the United States of America
Distributed in the United States and Canada by Publishers Group West
International Standard Book Number: 1-931382-02-6

10   9   8   7   6   5   4   3   2   1

Library of Congress Cataloging-in-Publication Data
Carmichael, Chris, 1960–
    The CTS collection : training tips for cyclists and triathletes /
    Carmichael Training Systems, featuring Chris Carmichael ;
    foreword by Lance Armstrong.
        p. cm.
    Includes index.
    ISBN 1-931382-02-6
       1. Cycling—Training. 2. Triathlon—Training. 1. Carmichael
    Training Systems. II. Title.

GV1048 .C37 2001
796.6'2—dc21   2001045515

Cover photos of Lance Armstrong by Graham Watson.
Cover photo of Conrad Stoltz (front, inset) by Galen Nathanson.

VeloPress
1830 N. 55th Street
Boulder, Colorado 80301-2700 USA
303/440-0601; Fax 303/444-6788
E-mail velopress@7dogs.com

To purchase additional copies of this book or other VeloPress
books, call 800/234-8356 or visit us on the Web at velopress.com.

Cover design and interior design by Rebecca Finkel

To athletes and coaches

who regard knowledge

as one of their greatest tools

CONTENTS

Foreword by *Lance Armstrong* ix

Introduction 1

PART I: Coaching

        Introduction 7

1   Blending Mental and Physical Preparation 9

2   It All Starts with You 17

3   The Way to Victory 23

4   Juniors 101 29

5   Hurry Up and Wait! 35

6   Aiming Toward the Goal 39

7   Leave No Stone Unturned 45

8   Preparing for Paris 49

9   Focusing on Success 55

PART II: Technique

        Introduction 63

10 Run Like a Gazelle 67

11 Spin Doctor 71

12 Cycling for Faster Run Splits 75

13 Tactics for Draft-Legal Racing 79

14 Get Down, Get Down 85

15 Criterium Tactics 89

16 You Can't Win If You Don't Sprint 93

PART III: Training

	Introduction	101
17	Functional Strength Training for Triathletes	103
18	How Can You Resist?	109
19	The "Great Indoors"	113
20	Boosting Early-Season Fitness with Tempo Workouts	117
21	Seeing Is Believing	125
22	Are You Ready? Test Yourself	129
23	All Roads Lead to Roubaix	135
24	Road Trip	141
25	The Art of Field Sprinting	145

PART IV: Recovery

	Introduction	153
26	Back Off, Buddy	157
27	Fluid Dynamics	163
28	Mid-term Break	167
29	Recovering for Better Training	171
30	Strategic Recovery	177

| About the Authors | 184 |
| Index | 189 |

FOREWORD

LANCE ARMSTRONG

Coaching has been a critical part of my development. Since my beginnings in triathlon, I have always had someone to guide me through the ups and downs of training and competing. Through two decades of athletic competition, I have worked with a variety of people and gained invaluable knowledge from each of them. Coaches have different styles, different philosophies, and different ways of communicating, but in the end, a great coach is an essential asset for any athlete.

My coaches have helped me develop the physical and mental attributes that I now rely on for success in cycling and life. Chasing athletic dreams is a difficult journey, full of punishing workouts, demoralizing losses, and incredible personal accomplishments. A coach takes the journey right alongside you, encouraging you through the hard times and celebrating the good times. Along the way, the trust and friendship developed between coach and athlete is frequently put to the test. At times I have been angry at coaches, argued with them, and refused to listen to anything they said. To their credit, they stuck by me, knowing that my drive to succeed and the incredible demands of my chosen pursuit were the source of my frustration and anger. In the world of elite athletics, there are only a few people you can truly count on — your family, your closest friends, and your coach.

I can chronicle my history in sports by reviewing the list of coaches I have worked with. There were coaches from school, Chris MacCurdy from the City of Plano (Texas) Swim Club, and even Jim Hoyt from the Richardson Bike

Mart. When I was racing triathlons, there were hosts of people in Plano and beyond to call on for help. Coaching begins on the most basic level of an experienced athlete giving advice to a novice. From there it gets more sophisticated, and it needs to. As you move through the ranks of any given sport, the coaching you seek and receive must keep pace with your position in the sport.

Chris Carmichael was my first real cycling coach. He and I got along well from the start, and his total faith in my potential was a great boost to my confidence. He saw me as I was, a strong young athlete who could become a great athlete with the help of the most important of all training tools, knowledge. He taught me everything he knew and then sought more knowledge from the best coaches he could find. As I and the other athletes in the National Team Program (George Hincapie, Freddy Rodriguez, and Bobby Julich) progressed, Chris moved ahead with us. He was open to new ideas and new technologies. Thus, the programs he developed for us helped us become Olympians and professional athletes.

While I was racing the Tour du Pont and preparing for the 1992 Olympics in Barcelona, Chris introduced me to Jim Ochowicz, the team director for the Motorola Professional Cycling Team. "Och" would become one of my greatest assets, as well as one of my closest friends. Coaching encompasses all aspects of sport, not merely fitness. Och was there through the first years of my professional career, teaching me about the culture of European cycling and guiding me around the pitfalls that bedevil so many young athletes. Both he and Chris were there when I finished dead last, far off the back, in my first professional race, the Classica San Sebastian. Their support helped me see beyond that dismal day and focus on what lay ahead.

As I indicated previously, coaches stick by you through thick and thin. During my cancer treatments, Chris and Och were at my bedside with my family and close friends. When I said that I was going to race again, they were two of the very few people who truly believed I could do it. It took over a year, a lot of trial and error, and a great deal of ingenuity and creativity, but by 1998, I thought I was ready to race again. My body was ready to compete, but I didn't know if I wanted to spend my time suffering through the hard life of professional cycling.

Shortly after returning to Europe with the Postal Service Cycling Team, I quit and flew back to Texas. I told Chris I was done, that I didn't want to race anymore, ever. He flew to Austin, and we talked about my decision. He didn't try to push me back into cycling; we just talked. Together we decided I would race again, but the U.S. professional championships in Philadelphia would be my last race, then I would retire. The story has been told many times by now, about the rainy training camp with Chris and Bob Roll in Boone, North Carolina; indeed, that trip helped me realize how much I loved this sport and that yes, I did want to be a professional cyclist. Fourteen months later, on the Champs-Elysées, my coaches, — Chris, Och, and my newest teacher, Johan Bruyneel—were there again, this time to celebrate the greatest accomplishment of our very long journey.

Successful coaches draw from resources beyond themselves, and I have benefited greatly because Chris, Och, Johan, and others continued to seek knowledge and try new ideas. It is wonderful to see that the coaching I have benefited from is now available to everyone through Chris's coaching company, Carmichael Training Systems. When CTS was still just an idea, Chris and I had talked about the concept of providing coaching services to the public. During that conversation, we had the exciting realization that everything Chris had learned through the years of working with elite athletes applied to athletes of all abilities. Not only would the training techniques and the workouts be suitable for anyone, but also the support system provided by a coach would be even more important for an athlete struggling to fit an athletic pursuit into an already busy life.

Since CTS started, I have seen proof that what we talked about that day is true. A close friend of mine in Austin, Morris Denton, signed up for a coaching package with CTS in fall 2000. Morris has a full-time career that involves a lot of traveling, and he and his wife, Laurie, have a two-year-old daughter named Lila. When Morris started working with his CTS Coach, Jim Rutberg, he was 225 pounds and struggling to finish training rides in Austin with me and a few others. While I spent the winter training in several locations, Morris stayed in Austin and trained with a schedule built around his business trips and family obligations. Even though he had less than ten hours a week to devote to training, he was a very different athlete when I saw him in spring 2001. He had lost 25 pounds and was looking very fit. While riding comfortably on a training ride with me, he explained that his next goal was to ride the masters criterium at the Ride for the Roses in Austin, Texas. Then, in accordance with his coach's program, Morris turned back for home while I continued on. He had come a long way that day; he used to turn around much sooner on our rides. More important, Morris had come a long way as an athlete in the months since we had ridden together. He hadn't had to sacrifice time away from his family or career, because he and his coach used his time more efficiently.

Every time I come home to Austin, a few more of my friends tell me they are working with CTS coaches. Chris tells me that new members and new coaches are pouring in every day. I think it's terrific. People should not underestimate the positive impact a coach can have on their lives. Every great athlete I have met during my career, from Eddy Merckx and Miguel Indurain to the emerging talent on the U.S. U23 (under 23) National Team, has or has had a coach. Bringing coaching to everyone means giving more people the chance to achieve their potential. There are good athletes out there who can become great champions with the same kind of coaching that I received. I look forward to meeting them.

INTRODUCTION

CHRIS CARMICHAEL

I am a fortunate man. I began my career traveling the world as an amateur and professional athlete before discovering coaching as a way to help other athletes achieve their potential. Over the years, I have had the pleasure of working with some of the finest athletes in the world, and I have learned from all of them. What worked for me as an athlete sometimes worked for others, but my coaching philosophy evolved from my experiences; a process that continues to this day.

I have worked with some athletes from the time they were just beginners, and I have had the opportunity to grow as a coach as they grew as athletes. The demands on both athletes and coaches have increased greatly over the past twenty years, and coaching sophistication has expanded to meet those demands. We now have the technology to see an accurate snapshot of an athlete's fitness on a day-to-day basis. But with the widespread availability of heart rate monitors and power meters, the expertise of a coach has become even more integral to an athlete's success. Analysis of information, combined with experience, enables coaches to create unique and challenging programs for their athletes.

For most of my coaching career, I worked only with elite athletes. Prescribing and monitoring their training, as well as fostering their emotional and psychological development, required a great deal of creativity. A program that brought one athlete to the next level often left the next exhausted and demoralized. Athletes respond differently to training, and the workouts and physical stress affect their emotional state. As a coach, I had to find ways to build programs based on sound physiological principles that would also match the personality and demeanor of the athlete. Pushing athletes to their limit isn't always the most effective means of producing great performances. Some athletes respond well to pressure, others crack. Some athletes need regular doses of confidence-building activities, while others have confidence to spare.

With the creation of Carmichael Training Systems, I now have the opportunity to coach athletes of all abilities. Because training is the primary focus of their lives, elite athletes are easy to coach. It is far more challenging to coach people with full-time jobs and families because their training must be integrated into an already busy lifestyle. These days I work with athletes ranging in age from 19 to 72, and the increased variety of training goals challenges me to grow as a coach.

One of the goals of CTS is to make world-class coaching available to athletes of all levels in a wide variety of sports. To this end, we have brought together coaches from around the United States and the world, giving them the opportunity to share ideas, philosophies, and techniques. As a result, we are creating a more diverse and educated community of dedicated coaches. Web-based technology enables CTS coaches to work with athletes anywhere in the world. Many coaches who were working part-time with a few athletes in their hometowns are now working as full-time coaches with CTS.

I have seen the positive impact a coach can have in an athlete's life and performance. In the past, coaching was available only to accomplished athletes, leaving countless others struggling to excel. The next generation of great athletes is waiting to be discovered and nurtured. Greater access to talented and dedicated coaches will help more of them achieve their goals.

This book will serve as a resource for athletes and coaches at all levels of sport. CTS coaches and athletes have published articles in *VeloNews* and *Inside Triathlon* magazines for several years. These magazines have given CTS the opportunity to present ideas drawn from the collective expertise of some of the finest coaches and athletes I have worked with. The most important thing I would like you to remember as you read this book, or any other, is that satisfaction with your performance should not come down to wins and losses, but should be born of progress. Find good information, use it wisely, and consult those with the knowledge and experience to help you. It is a simple idea, but it works for me as an athlete and a coach, and it will work for you too.

PART ONE

COACHING

Lance Armstrong wins stage 10 of the 2001 Tour de France atop Alp d'Huez. He feigned exhaustion most of the day before launching a decisive attack just after the start of the Tour's most fabled ascent.

INTRODUCTION TO COACHING

JIM LEHMAN

I hope that at some point in your athletic career, you had a coach who had a positive impact on your life. This person may have been a middle school soccer coach or a high school basketball coach, and to this day, the thought of that person makes you smile. Perhaps you did not realize at the time how important this person was, but once you had a chance to reflect, you discovered how much influence this person had on you. This person helped shape who you are today and probably taught you some very important lessons. Chances are good that this person had a similar guiding individual during his or her athletic career, someone who gave your coach the tools to become a successful athlete, just as your coach later imparted knowledge to you.

The common perception is that a coach is simply a person who trains athletes or organizes the game plan for a team. This definition is too limited. An effective coach must be more dynamic than this. The goal of coaching is to help others increase their performance, but how this is accomplished is different with each athlete. Successful coaches must be able to communicate effectively and frequently. In addition, they must possess clarity, competence, and confidence. Coaches help others look within themselves and achieve goals that they may not have been able to achieve alone. In doing so, coaches are able to connect with people on an individual level and address their specific needs. It is unfair to expect each athlete to respond identically or even for the same athlete to respond the same way each time. Just because a technique worked once does not mean it will work again; coaches must be able to adapt to the individual as well as to the situation.

A Chinese proverb holds that a teacher can open a door, but the students must pass through alone. Coaching involves a very similar principle: A coach can give individuals the tools to become better athletes, but ultimately the individuals must put this knowledge into action and make the decision to become better athletes. Thus, a coach cannot give athletes confidence; rather, athletes gain confidence through their experiences with the coach. As the training process evolves, they will be able to look forward to the next challenge with the knowledge that they are well prepared for the journey, and this knowledge gives them the assurance that they are capable of conquering successive obstacles.

Listen to the teachers in your life and take advantage of the opportunities to learn. Through this process you will develop the ability to acquire the knowledge and skills to improve your performance and achieve your goals.

BLENDING MENTAL AND PHYSICAL PREPARATION

C H R I S   C A R M I C H A E L

I t was mid-December as I boarded an airplane in Colorado Springs to head south to Austin, Texas, where I planned to spend a few days with Lance Armstrong as he sorted out his goals for the upcoming racing season.* These days I spend with Lance are valuable, as we discuss his goals and strategies. This is the mental process that will anchor and cement his desires and commitment to his training and racing program for 1999.

My journey as Lance's coach has led me to realize the critical importance of the mental process that all successful athletes need to experience. Throughout a lifetime in cycling as an athlete, coach, and administrator, I have seen some athletes become world champions and others, equally talented, never fulfill their athletic potential. Why? I believe they never properly blended the various mental aspects necessary to be successful into their physical training programs.

Empowering athletes to realize that they determine the outcome of their own cycling success is not always easy. This mental process must be integrated into the training programs that shape their bodies, the techniques that enhance their skills, and the tactical awareness that leads them to winning races. This is

* This article first appeared in slightly different form in *VeloNews.*

a deep, holistic approach that doesn't separate the mental from the physical factors of success but rather blends each into athletes' daily training programs and into the mental aspects that govern their mind-set. I have used this ongoing, interconnected approach to performance through the years I have been involved with cycling, athletes, and coaching.

Desire

Success starts with your desires that drive you to conquer your goals. Lance desires to wear the leader's yellow jersey in the Tour de France. Before he steps into action, he will assess his current ability to meet his desired goals. I like to have athletes ask themselves, "With regard to where I want to be, where am I now?" As you answer this, think outside of the box. Aim for the big picture in order to break the mold we all fall into as daily routines govern our lives.

True assessment means you need to examine your actions from a different perspective. For example, I have had numerous athletes tell me something like this: "Two years ago, I did only long, slow miles at this time of the year and I was flying, but now I can't get out of my own way"— or some other variation but with the same theme. These athletes are not riding poorly simply because they are riding long, slow miles. They are in a routine rut, doing the same thing year in and year out. They think that because the routine worked once, it will work again and again and again, but things change. Many factors affect how our physical and mental mind-set will respond to training. So what should these athletes do? They must step outside of the normal way they assess their training. They need to apply a different perspective to themselves, to analyze where they want to go and how they plan to get there. Once this is accomplished, a new training picture can take shape. Athletes must realize that new factors must be considered as a training program is being constructed and that they must be open to new forms of training if they expect to continue to be successful.

Make Your Own Rules

Cycling performance is not a science. There is no cookbook for success — no "If I do steps, a, b, and c, then I will win a World Championship Title." No such luck. We are all individuals and are governed by different rules that shape our bodies and motivate our minds. There is no single way to do something. You make the rules about the right way, or the wrong way, to get to where you want to go.

Early in 1998, it appeared that Lance would limit his participation in stage racing, events contested over several consecutive days or weeks. At the time, it seemed there could be some physical reasons why he wouldn't be successful in stage racing. He worked with his team of advisers, including U.S. Postal Service Cycling's team management, Jim Ochowicz, and me, to devise a new racing plan. We changed the rules on how Lance played the game. During March, April, and May, Lance raced fewer than a dozen times. This was not the tried-and-true approach, but in his first race in Europe, he won. Lance made his own rules and was stage racing with greater success than he had ever before achieved. Before you can chase your desires, you must know exactly what they are and where you are in relation to them. You must also have the courage to make your own rules and not be governed by perceived limitations.

The Power to Choose Your Goals

The winter months are a good time to reflect on the past season. From the data you accumulate, you will determine your desires, make your rules, and have the power to choose your goals and prospects for the coming year. The goals you set now will define your entire program for the rest of the year. These goals will have many different time frames and degrees of attainability.

Dream Goals

At the top end of the goal spectrum are "dream goals," ultimate goals that push the limits of what is possible for you. Dream goals go hand-in-hand with the physical process of peaking for your season's most important competition. Dream goals are a great motivating factor as your body is beginning to enter peak conditioning for achieving new heights of excellence. Hence, it's important to nurture that motivation through the creation of dream goals that are long shots but possible if everything falls into place. These goals can help you through tough times and also serve as food for fantasy on long rides.

A dream goal for Lance could be reaching the podium at the finish of the Tour de France. Of course, this is the highest goal in all of cycling. So even as a dream goal, it's only suitable to an athlete of Lance's caliber. For someone who has been a category 4 racer for three years, finishing races in the main group, a dream goal might be to win several local races and upgrade to a category 3.

Write down your dream goal and refer back to it regularly to remind yourself where you're going and what the ultimate prize is.

Mid-Term Goals

After dream goals are mid-term goals. These goals will often be the end points of a training cycle. Before tackling your mid-term goals, you should have sufficiently developed important physical qualities that will make you competitive in your races. This is where you focus your efforts on achieving something realistic but ambitious. For instance, early in 1998, Lance set his sights on a top-20 placing in the Ruta del Sol. He reached this goal, which gave him a confidence boost that enabled him to push through difficult periods in the spring. Lance's experience clearly shows the marriage between the physical and mental process of an ultimate performance. These mid-term goals are confidence builders that help push you into the peaking process of the cycling season. Without these goals, you would head into the heart of the season with little confidence. Desire, commitment, and preparation would slowly dissipate, as would your physical attributes.

Micro Goals

On a daily or weekly basis, it's important to have micro goals that focus your energy during each ride or week of riding. These micro goals create a common thread that ties your daily workouts to your mid-term goals and provides a daily link to your dream goals. When Lance sets out on a ride in the morning, he has an explicit list of goals — often a specific number of intervals, a minimum mileage, a specific heart rate, or a particular skill he wants to develop. Some days he may work on maintaining a specific heart rate and pedal cadence while climbing; other days he may focus on developing his sprinting or descending skills.

Constantly evaluate your progress in reaching micro goals. This assessment will help you turn goal setting into an ongoing process that moves you forward in your daily workouts. I have seen many athletes become good at establishing a dream goal, but they get sidetracked and never reach their goals because they have turned goal setting into a static process. This daily evaluation should be integrated into your training program because changes in you, and many other factors, require modification of your daily workouts. This adaptability keeps your goals from being set in stone. Planning is always an ongoing endeavor. Things change on a daily basis: Races get canceled, weather affects your training, you get sick or injured. The only way to stay on top of the changes is to change along with them.

Visualization

During his workouts leading up to the 1993 world championships, Lance said that he would "see" every detail of the last few laps of the race — right down to the gear in which he was attacking the breakaway. He was visualizing.

Visualization is part of integrating your goals into your workouts. Visualization, or mental imagery, while training helps top athletes see themselves performing at their peak. You are setting a mental stage for a great performance. The process helps you become familiar with performing strongly before racing . See yourself racing, perhaps one of your mid-term goals, before you participate in the event. Visualize every detail of your racing performance being perfect. Small details such as gear shifts, pedal cadence, and body position should appear vividly. These details will help you translate visualization into reality. When visualizing your goals, you can mentally see, hear, and feel the performance. Use all your senses in this imagery process as a way to become prepared for the sensations associated with achieving your goals. This engages your thoughts, emotions, and feelings and, more important, blends your daily workouts into your goals.

Blending your mental preparation into your physical training encompasses all aspects that affect cycling performance and molds these into a holistic approach that handles the real-life training and racing scenarios every athlete faces.

During the 2001 Tour de France, Lance Armstrong demonstrated his ability to excel in the time trials as well as the mountains.

CHAPTER 2

IT ALL STARTS WITH YOU

CHRIS CARMICHAEL

hat are your strengths and weaknesses as a cyclist?* The real answers may surprise you. It's easy to convince yourself that time trialing is your niche, or that you're best suited for climbing. Of course, once you've made an assumption of this sort, it's natural to focus your training around your self-diagnosed strengths. Yet it may well be that you're better suited for something entirely different. In that case, your focus on the wrong skill could be a powerful disservice to your true potential.

The mind rules the body; it dictates how we train and what results will satisfy us. So the first step to improved performance is the realization that success begins with you—and your brain! It is imperative that you understand the mind-body connection and how it will cause you to perform in a manner that is consistent with your self-image. In order to alter your performances, you may have to alter your self-image.

We all hold beliefs about ourselves. These convictions are often a result of our positive or negative history—comments or performances that occurred and reinforced our self-image. For example, let's say you routinely finish climbs off

* This article first appeared in slightly different form in *VeloNews* 29, no. 2 (2000).

the back on group rides. You're not a climber, right? Maybe. Or perhaps you simply aren't training correctly or sufficiently in this area. The first challenge is to deconstruct the self-image so that you can properly determine your strengths.

To "start with a clean sheet" means you have no limitations. Because our own mental barriers prevent us from performing to our maximum, we must remove these barriers. This will assist us in correctly diagnosing our true abilities so that we can take steps to improve the areas that could cost us victory.

Record Keeping

The task of identifying your strengths and weaknesses and tracking your progress begins with record keeping—and for that purpose, a good logbook is an indispensable ally. Logging your training enables you to track how you felt before, during, and after rides; the heart-rate zones you targeted; the weather conditions; the route you took; and other variables. Some riders use printed logbooks; others prefer computers. The key is to develop the habit of consistently recording the data you'll need in order to review your training.

Many top professional athletes keep a training journal throughout their careers. I coach Lance Armstrong, who has kept one since his early training years as a junior. These are valuable records to help both of us understand his body and how it responds to training. I like to refer to training journals as "personal performance logs." In my coaching, I have found them to be a valuable training tool for any athlete.

At Carmichael Training Systems (CTS), we have developed a software program that serves as a training journal, giving us plenty of Lance's physiological test results, workouts, race results, and biofeedback information.

This information is stored in my computer, and I can compare it against the workouts I prescribed for him. The program greatly enhances record keeping and helps a coach easily recall and evaluate an athlete's progress.

It is important to measure and quantify what you want to improve. A regular timed course ridden at the same perceived level of effort can show you where you are in relation to your fitness goals — and in relation to where you are in your training season. The course style depends on the area of targeted improvement but can range from a flat loop to a point-to-point hill climb. If you want to improve your sprint, a good benchmark may be a timed A-to-B sprint, perhaps even with a consistent flying start. If you own a power meter such as the SRM or the Tune Power-Tap, recording a regular training loop, a long climb, or a specific field test will give you an objective and repeatable measurement.

As you look back in your daily training journal, you will see signs that lead to identifying and modifying workouts. This should be done before digging yourself into a training hole.

What to Look For

1. *Ability to reach prescribed heart rate training intensities.* If you are having trouble reaching or maintaining them, consider reducing the training intensity or training volume. You may also need to evaluate fluid intake and be on the lookout for signs of dehydration. In addition, you should review your training data to ensure that you're including ample recovery time following workouts.

2. *Sleeping habits.* Recording sleeping habits can help you evaluate the training load. If you notice a change in your sleeping habits, you may need

to reduce your training load. Poor sleep could be caused by training fatigue or muscle soreness.

3. *Behavioral markers.* After workouts, verbal interaction between you and others can help identify behavioral patterns. I look for changes in a person's normal behavior. Generally, if I see signs of apathy, poor concentration, or irritability during conversations, I will evaluate the current training to see if I need to reduce its intensity or volume.

4. *Morning pulse.* Establish the practice of taking your waking heart rate while lying quietly in bed. If your morning pulse is three to five beats higher or lower than your average waking pulse, this could be an indication that you are fatigued, overtrained, or coming down with an illness.

5. *Body weight.* Before beginning a morning workout, it is important to weigh yourself. This should be done at the same time daily, preferably just after waking. Recording this data helps you quickly notice any change in weight. Weight loss of more than one pound a week can lead to fatigue or other problems.

The purpose of these processes is to find benchmarks through which you can measure your training responses that lead to increased performance. In the long term, the habit of regularly recording training and periodically measuring your performance will create a model of your personal performance. You can review the logs to see how your performance was affected when, for example, you tried different training methods, or if you caught the flu, how long it was before you were back up to snuff. Personal performance logs provide a wealth of information that can be used to establish strengths and identify weaknesses.

When you build a personal performance log, keep in mind that results in training will differ from those in the heat of competition. Lance Armstrong, for example, reaches his maximum sustainable training intensity at a heart rate of about 185 beats per minute (bpm) for 30 minutes; in competition, however, he can maintain a heart rate of more than 190 bpm for well over an hour. This variance in maximum effort between the training and racing contexts is found in competitive cyclists of all levels.

Overcoming Mental Barriers

Early in Lance's career, he was told he could be a great one-day racer but would never be competitive in the grand tours. To be superior at one-day racing is certainly an admirable gift, and many a career has been built around it. However, Lance isn't particularly fond of being told what he can't do, nor is he eager to succumb to any imposed limitations.

After his recovery from cancer, Lance had lost a great deal of upper-body mass. More important, however, was how he worked on increasing his pedal speed, learning to climb with better form, and developing a new mental outlook. Through these efforts, Lance improved his competitive position significantly. The 1998 Vuelta a Espana was an eye-opener for the cycling world, as well as an important mid-term confidence builder for Lance. His fourth-place finish disproved the doubters heard early in his career. It also

proved that targeting specific skill areas for improvement is always effective—
even for professionals at the peak of the sport. Lance started 1999 with a
"clean sheet": He had a new self-image that didn't impose limits.

Remember, too, that although mid-term goals are a critical part of any
long-term pursuit, they are also achievements to be celebrated in their own
right. Sure, Lance's fourth-place finish showed him that he was on the right
track and could be fully competitive in the grand tours. But fourth place in
the Vuelta is a major milestone in itself. It's fine to use mid-term goals as
markers toward long-term objectives, as long as you appreciate what you've
accomplished along the way.

• • • •

Training is a constant challenge, and fine-tuning your regimen to
meet your goals can take a great deal of effort. Regular measurement of your
performance, in combination with accurate record keeping in a personal
performance log, will help you identify your strengths and target your
weaknesses. Use this information to create a self-image that isn't limited
by your past actions and performances. The time is always right to start
with a clean sheet.

CHAPTER 3

THE WAY TO VICTORY

CHRIS CARMICHAEL

s the off-season comes to a close, our athletes at CTS have achieved strength gains from a solid weight program and on-the-bike resistance workouts.* They have also developed better pedaling mechanics from fixed-gear workouts.

In addition, each athlete has developed specific goals for the season. Lance Armstrong wants a repeat victory at the Tour de France and an Olympic gold medal. George Hincapie is shooting for a podium finish at Paris-Roubaix. Matt Kelly and Jess Swiggers are bound for the UCI (Union Cicliste Internationale) mountain-bike World Cup circuit. Master cyclists Andy Muldoon and Manny Lopez are aiming for medals at the road nationals.

Goals and events may vary dramatically, but every athlete needs a detailed plan to reach peak performance as major milestones approach. It is the coach's job to create that plan before developing specific training programs for his or her athletes.

* This article first appeared in slightly different form in *VeloNews*.

The Role of a Coach

Many sports organizations develop task statements to describe the role the coach is expected to play. One of my favorites is from the British Cycling Federation. It states that a coach "enables the athlete to achieve levels of performance to a degree that may not have been possible if left to his/her own endeavors." George Dyson took this statement one step further while speaking to the nineteenth session of the International Olympic Academy in Greece in 1979: "The wise coach develops not only the fullest physical potential in his charges, but also those capacities and habits of mind and body which enrich and ennoble their later years." This concept pushes the role of the coach well beyond merely preparing an athlete for competition.

I like to create the right environment for learning, one in which the athlete understands the methods and reasons behind the prescribed training. This approach elicits better "buy-in" from the athlete and more reason for the athlete to provide valuable feedback on the effectiveness of the training program. Most athletes are highly motivated, but motivation can vary greatly based upon their recent results and performances. The task, therefore, is to help them maintain a high level of enthusiasm and excitement—even when things aren't going quite right and their performance is not what they had expected.

Coaches take on many roles, ranging among facilitator, adviser, motivator, instructor, assessor, friend, mentor, organizer, chauffeur, fact finder . . . and the bottomless pit of being someone who knows a little something of just about everything!

The Attack Plan

Building an annual training program is a core task that a coach must perform. It requires some key information, which can be obtained by developing a model through which an athlete will progress. Each level of development should build upon another, until an athlete arrives at the top fully ready to achieve his or her personal goals.

The six-level model we have developed at CTS incorporates all the components necessary for achieving peak performance:

- Goal setting
- Physical training
- Skill development
- Confidence building
- Peaking activities
- 100 percent readiness, mentally, physically, and technically

This model recasts various forms of athlete development into six conceptual levels, but all aspects are integrated by the coach. For example, I begin by incorporating each athlete's personal goals into his or her physical training.

Take George Hincapie: If he is to place in the top three in Paris-Roubaix, then the workouts and training I prescribe for him must adequately prepare him for the demands of this event. Put another way, before I can build his training plan, I must determine exactly what he is training for.

First come the energy demands. Paris-Roubaix can last seven hours, so George must have a large aerobic capacity. If he can use his aerobic system to supply the majority of the power required, he will burn fewer carbohydrates and produce fewer negative by-products such as lactic acid.

In addition, Paris-Roubaix demands that an athlete produce extreme bursts of power to close the gaps when groups splinter over the cobblestone sections. During one critical period of the 1999 race, Hincapie bridged a large gap to the lead group of riders. This effort required him to ride within eight beats per minute of his maximum heart rate for close to four minutes. To ensure that he can sustain that level of effort, his anaerobic engine must be trained at the same time as his aerobic power and endurance.

Skills are the next part of the equation. A race like Paris-Roubaix means hours of practice to build coordination, mobility, and agility and to guarantee that bike-handling skills are finely tuned. George will accomplish this with a steady diet of racing: By the time he reaches this year's Paris-Roubaix, he will have at least 20 races in his legs. He'll also sharpen his coordination on the bike to a fine edge with a precompetition training ride three or four days before the classic. As he rides the last 100 kilometers of the practice ride, his brain will absorb each aspect of these critical kilometers, noting the best lines to take. He'll also etch the significant landmarks into his mind, so he can recognize each cobblestone section and recall its level of difficulty.

Before the race, the U.S. Postal Service Team director will develop a racing strategy. Together, the riders and the director will examine the strengths and weaknesses of the other teams as well as their own and will consider how weather conditions could affect their strategy. Rain would create slippery conditions, making the cobblestones even more dangerous. Normally, this means that the race will begin early in the day, so early breakaway attempts cannot be counted out. George's tactics during the race will be developed with input from his teammates and director and will be honed by his own racing instincts derived from the best method of all: race, race, and race some more.

All those races leading up to Paris-Roubaix provide a great opportunity for George to snag some good results — and build his confidence. After all, what could help more than a stage win in Paris-Nice or a top-five finish in Milan–San Remo? At the same time, such a result would help George keep a strong commitment as he forges onward to Paris-Roubaix. Strong commitment is key. Without it, an athlete can be easily sidetracked from a training program and lose focus.

By the week of Paris-Roubaix, George should feel powerful and confident in his fitness. His tactics will be razor sharp and he will be nearly ready. Peaking for an event cannot happen if earlier training goals have not been met. These goals should have supplied plenty of "overload" in the areas of endurance, power, and strength. If this strategy has been followed properly, then a reduction in George's training and/or racing load at this time will allow him to freshen up and spring to an extremely high level of fitness. Two days out, his energy will soar—to the point that he feels as if he's crawling out of his skin. With his daily training reduced, George's main task now will be to fight his desire to continue training long hours. Most of his time must be spent relaxing around the hotel and waiting for the race.

When race day arrives, George should be 100 percent ready — physically, mentally, and technically. A great result, however, is never guaranteed. Despite meticulous preparation, many things are beyond the control of George's team, managers, mechanics, coach, and even George himself. But if his training program has been on target and followed, and if he arrives at the starting line feeling his own readiness, George will be one giant step closer to reaching his goal: a podium finish at the Queen of the Classics, Paris-Roubaix.

CHAPTER 4

JUNIORS 101
Stuff I Wish I Knew Then

MATT KELLY

L ast year, while racing as a junior, I was fortunate to be on the Devo team.* The team worked well for me and, I think, for the other juniors, because we didn't feel pressure to get results. At the races, I was comfortable being around people my age, and all the logistics of racing were taken care of. That enabled me to concentrate on getting myself ready for the race, and that kind of focus is extremely important.

No matter what team you're on, however, there are a few things that are key to any junior's success. Most important is to keep a balance between your racing and your life. Racing should be fun: You need to be serious about your goals, but you have to enjoy it, too. John Kemp, who runs the Devo program, says he's looking for drive and fun when he selects riders for his team. Here are a few ways to find that balance.

Priorities

First, you need to set priorities—figure out how much time you can or want to devote to cycling. Whatever you decide, be sure cycling is what you really want,

* This article first appeared in slightly different form in *VeloNews* 29, no. 4 (2000).

and that the reason you're doing it is for yourself. Once you have that figured out, set goals; it seems to me that too many people don't have a clear idea of what they want to achieve.

Goals should be specific and cover everything from ultimate goals — like winning the world championships — to daily goals that help you keep your focus. A season with peaks and valleys and one or two great results is better than one with all mediocre results. The best time to plan your seasonal goals is before the season begins. Set a series of medium-range goals that you can achieve and that will let you know you're on your way to the big one.

It is also important to set measurable, achievable daily goals, because these small steps will bring you within reach of your larger goal. Every day, write down a couple of tasks you would like to accomplish in training, and do your best to complete them. Your goal could be to reach 182 bpm heart rate during your last interval or to average 19 mph for the entire ride. Visualization is an important and effective way to help you reach your goals. For example, during intervals when you're sprinting, imagine in the last 100 meters that you're on your way to winning the nationals or the world championships.

Have a Coach

Just as important as having goals is having a coach. I wish I had had one during my earlier years as a junior. On a couple of occasions, I've faded before the nationals, just when I wanted to be at my best. I think a coach would have helped me make it to nationals fresher and in good shape. This ties in directly to keeping a training diary as well: You can learn from your mistakes, and a coach can help you learn what you did wrong and how to do it right the next time.

The best thing about having a coach is that you have a mentor who can help you stay focused on your goals. My coach, Chris Carmichael at CTS, has been instrumental in helping me achieve my goals, primarily by giving me confidence in my abilities.

You need someone who can stand back and see things you can't see on your own, such as overtraining. Listen to your parents because they can help with some of that evaluation. They know you well, so they can tell you when you're getting edgy or not being yourself. Yet having a parent as your only coach usually isn't the best idea, because—of course—kids don't want to listen to their parents. That's why it's good to have a coach you can talk to and who can give you objective advice.

Laid-Back Genes

As for my parents, I was fortunate to have the most supportive and least uptight parents anyone could have. Cycling is best when the motivation comes from within, not from an overly excited parent. I've seen some extreme cases of kids who don't even want to ride their bikes and do badly in their races. Afterward, the parents say, "You're riding home!" I feel bad for those kids, and I doubt they will stick with bike racing for long.

Stretch Every Day

Stretching is a huge part of staying healthy. I've seen people miss long stretches of the season because of injuries that could have been prevented by stretching. My dad has been telling me for years to stretch more. Ignoring his advice almost made me miss the cyclo-cross world championship race last year because my back was strained. My back still bothers me during races, and yet it's something I could have prevented with stretching.

Keep a Training Diary

A training diary will help you learn from what you did right and what you did wrong. The information you gather allows you to learn more about yourself, and you train smarter as you learn.

Be as specific as possible: Write down your mileage, heart rate (waking and during the ride), terrain, what workouts you did, how you felt physically and mentally, and anything that strikes you as notable about the day. Don't forget to write down your goals.

Do Other Sports

Cross-country running, soccer, and other sports at school are good for your overall fitness. They can also give you a valuable mental break, especially during the off-season. That way you don't limit yourself to being only a bike racer. In my case, running cross-country helped me become a better cyclo-crosser. The best part of my season was always when I was running cross-country.

Doing other sports also helps you develop your all-around aerobic system, so that you don't get too sport-specific early in your life. Don't be too discipline-specific during the season either. Mountain-bike racers should try road racing, and vice versa—and, of course, do cyclo-cross.

Know When It's Time to Get Serious

You can't be 100 percent focused the entire season; you'll fade before the important racing arrives. So pick your key events to peak for and do well in and then relax and have fun during the other races. Use them for fun, for working on your technical skills, but don't get too intense about races that aren't major goals on your program. Chris has told me that about eight weeks before the key event is when it's time to start paying close attention to what you're doing—such as getting to bed on time, eating well, and starting to employ visualization techniques.

Above all, you need to balance your life and racing. It's important to have a good time riding and racing, or you'll get frustrated and stop. Many things you can learn only first-hand: strategy, your physical limits, and the like. By setting goals in a variety of terms—short and long—you can measure your improvement and success. Hitting goals will keep you motivated to race and try even harder, and that's the key to sticking with it.

George Hincapie has been a strong man in the peloton, but the big victory had always eluded him. However, in 2001 he captured his first semi-classic win at Ghent-Wevelgem.

CHAPTER 5

HURRY UP AND WAIT!

Tapering for a Big Race
Needs Good Coach-Rider Communication

CHRIS CARMICHAEL

After a 45-minute phone stint talking with an athlete, you hang up and wonder: Have I done everything I can to get him ready?* Is she sufficiently fit? Can I squeeze a few more intervals into his schedules? Will extra intervals make her faster? Chances are, your athletes are wondering the same things, and they're looking to you for the answers.

The weeks leading up to a major competition are when a coach really proves his or her worth. The process of preparing athletes to compete at full capacity can become complicated: Too much intensity fries athletes, but too much rest leaves them lethargic. And, of course, different events and different cycling disciplines require very different coaching strategies.

The concept we are discussing here is called "tapering." Tapering is a transition from race-specific training to goal-fulfilling racing. Rest, fine-tuning of systems, and maintenance of existing strength are the goals for this short period. How much time? That depends on the length and type of event an athlete is preparing for.

Riders competing in shorter events need more time to taper than those competing in longer races. Track riders, some mountain-bike racers, downhillers,

* This article first appeared in slightly different form in *VeloNews* 29, no. 12 (2000).

and even criterium specialists fall into the first category. Their events last anywhere from one minute to two hours, which means there is no downtime, no time to feel sluggish. A kilo rider must come out of the blocks at full power, so preparation for the event should focus on retaining power and making it readily accessible.

During the last few weeks of preparation before a major competition, short-distance riders need to reduce their overall training volume and increase the intensity of the efforts they perform. The goal is to overload race-specific systems, without completely fatiguing the rider. Thus, some workouts should be of greater intensity than that required in a race. I often have track racers complete flying kilometers above race pace 12–14 days before their big event. As the event gets closer, I reduce the recovery time between efforts. Short, high-intensity intervals develop the body's ability to produce energy rapidly as soon as the event starts.

Events that last longer than two hours are a different animal altogether. These are endurance events, so maintaining endurance is key in the final preparation phase of training. Long-distance riders need less time to taper than do their short-distance counterparts. If they feel sluggish in the first hour of a five-hour road race, it's no big deal. They might start feeling terrific in the third hour and end up winning. It is important, however, for the long-distance rider to maintain the systems that support endurance cycling, including mechanisms for glycogen storage and fat utilization. If these mechanisms do not remain in top shape and begin to return to sedentary function, the athlete will not be able to compete at full capacity. I like to use a technique called "super-compensation," a technique I used with Lance Armstrong before the 1993 World Road Championship—which he won.

Under this training regimen, Lance had a long ride on Wednesday before the race on Sunday. The intensity was low to moderate with a few hill accelerations thrown in. Each hill acceleration lasted about a minute and raised his heart rate to about 95 percent of its maximum. The next few days' training consisted of short, low-intensity rides. This combination of rides depleted Lance's systems and storage levels while allowing enough time for him to recover completely.

With this kind of training, careful attention must be given to nutrition to ensure that there is adequate fuel to refill depleted reserves. The body reacts to the long workout and subsequent depletion by super-compensating, increasing its fuel reserves and anticipating another similar effort. The timing is crucial, because the super-compensation effect lasts only for a short time, and that time varies from athlete to athlete.

During the tapering period, communication is critical, as is a coach-athlete relationship built on trust and cooperation. Athletes must be made aware that they are not going to feel good or ready to race 10–14 days out. This gives them confidence, because even though they feel lousy, their coach has told them to expect that reaction. This advance knowledge reinforces that they can trust and should listen to their coach.

Charlie Walsh, head coach of the Australian track cycling team, once told me that he considers it a good sign when his athletes cannot ride their best race times 10 days before competition. However, athletes get frustrated and a bit scared when they do not feel in top shape and their event is just around the corner. If the communication between coach and athlete is poor, this frustration and fear can have disastrous effects on an athlete's psyche.

Athletes tend to test themselves every day, on every training ride, as they approach an event. They are anxious about their form and want confirmation that they are ready. The problem is that this constant testing interferes with the training and preparation work they need to be doing. Some testing, in the form of field tests, tune-up races, or lab testing, is a good idea, as long as it is structured into the athlete's program. But the athlete needs to resist the urge to self-test constantly, because the effort wastes valuable energy. It's up to coaches to make their athletes understand why they must stick to their programs—and forgo self-testing.

Athletes are not the only ones who need to listen. Coaches need to hear and interpret clues and comments that reveal their athletes' well-being and then judge if they need more rest, more work, or a tension-breaker. I have found, especially working with entire teams of cyclists, that when people became irritable or argumentative, they were "telling" me they felt tired or overworked. This was my cue to reduce their training and give them more time to rest. Depending on the personality I was dealing with, I recommended some time alone or doing some activity they found relaxing—you know, bungee jumping, sky diving, swimming with sharks, the relaxing kind of stuff that has nothing to do with the athlete's upcoming race.

CHAPTER 6

AIMING TOWARD THE GOAL
How Lance Armstrong's Training Becomes More Specialized as the Tour Approaches

CHRIS CARMICHAEL

Foresight is perhaps the greatest benefit a coach can provide.* Failure to look far enough ahead can hinder an athlete's season or even his or her career. Whereas athletes must focus on the day-to-day tasks of taking care of themselves and their training, their coach needs to help them see beyond the next competition and achieve longer-term goals.

For Lance Armstrong, it is the coach's job to keep his focus on the season's major goal: winning the Tour de France for the second time. As he approached the final eight weeks of his preparation for the Tour, it was time to make the transition from the "preparation period" to the "specialization period."

Lance's preparation period focused on developing the energy systems essential for endurance sports. He spent hours training his aerobic system through long, steady rides, tempo workouts, and lactate-threshold workouts. He used this time to target these specific components of his cycling. By May, he needed to combine these components and arrive 100 percent ready at the Tour de France prologue on July 1.

In May, Lance entered the very important specialization period. This transitional time emphasizes the differences between training and competition. In training,

---

* This article first appeared in slightly different form in *VeloNews* 29, no. 10 (2000).

athletes have control over the intensity and duration of efforts. In competition, they must be ready and able to respond to unexpected challenges and put forth unprecedented effort. This requires the physical ability to use the body's energy systems and the mental ability to focus the mind and fully commit to the task at hand. A highly trained athlete transitions to a highly trained competitor during this specialization period.

Many coaches like to design an athlete-development model that will serve as a blueprint for constructing training programs and specific workouts. For Lance's training model, I use a pyramid design. It starts with Lance's goals—from, say, next week to five years down the road—and uses these goals as the base of his training. Each layer of the pyramid builds on the next, progressing through physical training, skill development, and confidence-building activities.

It is critical not to separate the mind and body as the coach develops an athlete, as both aspects are so closely linked that they must be "trained" in parallel. Separating the two leads to a strong but unfocused athlete, not a champion. As an athlete trains, he gains strength and the knowledge of his body's capabilities. And part of coaching is educating an athlete in the ways and means of using his physical and mental assets to achieve his goals.

At the pinnacle of Lance's training pyramid is the "100-percent-ready athlete." This is an athlete who has trained all of the energy systems, has met his racing demands, and is in top physical, mental, and emotional shape. He is rested, fresh, and positive. The 100-percent-ready athlete has the knowledge necessary to succeed and the self-esteem to believe in what he is doing.

I have found that a successful training program has a cumulative effect on Lance. The better he prepares, the more confidence he gains; and the more commitment Lance has, the more focused he is toward achieving his goal. Lance entered the specialization period knowledgeable, well trained, and with a positive outlook. Using the pyramid as our blueprint for training, Lance was ready for the final steps toward peak performance that would demand from him the greatest amounts of determination, confidence, and focused energy.

The specialization period can start 8–10 weeks before a major goal of the season. Most coaches begin by blending in competitions—integrating the variable demands of racing with those of structured training. Racing taxes the body in ways that training simply cannot. The rapid and unexpected changes in exertion, the commitment to do whatever it takes to stay in the breakaway, reach the next summit, or survive in the gutter, create bike racers from paperboys.

A race schedule during the specialization period must be strategically planned. The idea is to use competitions to fine-tune an athlete's fitness, hone his skills, and build his confidence. Overly hard races won't build fitness if the athlete can last only a third of the way before being dropped. Getting crushed in races doesn't exactly build confidence either. On the other hand, the events shouldn't be ridiculously easy. Races during the specialization period should be hard enough that they positively stress the athlete, challenge his skills, and stoke his competitive drive.

Athletes can benefit from a mid-term confidence builder. For Lance, the mid-April Amstel Gold Race— 10 weeks before the Tour—worked well in 1999. It has been a good event for him, and it suits his style of racing very well. This year, it didn't have the same effect—because he got caught behind a pileup at a critical juncture. However, a few days later, at the French Cup race, Paris-Camembert, Lance finished a close second — which helped drive his confidence to new heights.

A mid-term confidence builder like this decreases the pressure that comes with preparing for the Tour. The race complements Lance's training plan, refines his tactical and bike-handling skills, and helps him gauge his progress. The event need not be an easy race or a guaranteed win; Amstel Gold is certainly neither. It is essential that Lance has a good race, makes the right selections, and competes in the finale. A mid-term confidence builder should be an event in which an athlete can be competitive and finish with a feeling that he is right on schedule for his larger goal.

Training during the specialization period should be geared toward the specific demands of racing. This is when we add anaerobic work and sprints to prepare for breakaways and sprint finishes. Lance is now doing climbing repeats at lactate threshold and above. These workouts prepare him for the mountain stages of the Tour de France. In addition, he has begun time-trial training, to adapt to his TT position and to develop his power at lactate threshold.

The aerobic training is balanced with race simulation — which in Lance's case includes reconnaissance rides of several of this year's Tour stages. This has its pluses, particularly in building confidence and gaining knowledge of the terrain; but it also has its dangers—such as the crash Lance had in early May while descending a mountain road in the Pyrenees. Luckily, the crash occurred during his preparation — not in the Tour — and only set his training back a few days, instead of eliminating him from his season goal.

During this buildup period, aerobic-conditioning rides are needed to maintain aerobic fitness. But it's possible that an athlete's aerobic fitness will begin to drop as a result of an exceedingly high volume of intensive training.

An athlete like Lance, working toward a major goal, can be hard to stop, so he also needs to get plenty of rest.

Workouts above lactate threshold and approaching VO_2 max are hard on the system. Often an athlete starts to feel strong and fast, and since now he can ride faster, he does. Two weeks later, he is tired and beginning to ride slower. Why does this happen? Think of all the training as potential energy. We spend all this time gaining potential energy (strength, fitness, confidence, and drive) to accomplish our goal. If we use all that energy before the event, how much energy will we have left when we really need it?

A coach has but one goal: to help each athlete develop into the 100-percent-ready athlete. The specialization period is an essential step in that process because it sharpens the focus of training to a singular point. The 100-percent-ready athlete may not always win, but arriving on the starting line in top physical and mental shape means there are fewer things that can get in your way as you head to the finish line.

CTS training helped Dylan Casey earn a stage win in the 2000 Tour of Luxembourg and become a member of the 2000 U.S. Olympic cycling team.

CHAPTER 7

LEAVE NO STONE UNTURNED
The Coach and the Athlete: Who Does What?

CHRIS CARMICHAEL

By the time Olympians make it to the big show, they have probably been competitive athletes for the majority of their life.* They're used to big events. But the Olympic games are different from any other competition in the world. The scope of the event is enormous. The number of athletes, fans, and media is overwhelming. Some of the most experienced athletes get flustered and make mistakes that they normally wouldn't. Preparing athletes to cope with the distractions and stresses of race day is one of a coach's most critical tasks.

Come Prepared

A vital part of preparing for a major event is gathering information on the event itself. The day of the race is not the time to learn the length of the course, the severity of the climbs, the start time, or the normal local weather conditions. A coach must gather this information as far in advance as possible, as it may alter the way an athlete is prepared. It is important to teach athletes to research the

---

* This article first appeared in slightly different form in *VeloNews* 29, no. 16 (2000).

course before the start. When does feeding begin and end? Where is the feed zone? Is it on a hill or flat ground? What does the final kilometer look like?

Athletes must realize the finish area will look different at the end of the race. The crowd, the barriers, and especially the speed of the approach will make distance difficult to judge. Teach athletes to use distinctive, immovable objects as landmarks within the final 10 kilometers. Buildings, traffic islands, crosswalks, and bridges work well. Does the race end with circuits, or do you see the finish line only once?

A dress rehearsal can be a valuable experience. This is especially true for events requiring special equipment: time trials and some track events, for example. In the weeks prior to the Olympics, Lance Armstrong will do a few race simulations in all of his time-trial gear, including his aerodynamic Giro helmet, a skinsuit, and shoe covers. He will eat and warm up the same way he will in Sydney.

It is always a good idea to use new equipment in training before trying it in competition. In the 1984 Olympic games in Los Angeles, one of the favorites for the individual kilometer time trial wore a brand-new aerodynamic helmet in competition. During his event, the helmet slid down over his eyes, and he had to adjust it as he rode. After months and years of training, that simple mistake took him out of medal contention.

Making a List, Checking It Twice

Packing, eating, traveling, and warming up are easy enough at a local road race, but the pressure is exponentially increased at district, national, and world championship events, as well as the Olympics. Haphazard race preparation almost guarantees something will go wrong. By race day, the routine should be so ingrained that only a natural disaster could distract an athlete from getting ready to race.

Use a checklist when packing your race bag. Determine what pre-race meal works best for you and how long before the race you need to eat it. Don't change your pre-race meal before an important event. If you are traveling by airplane, pack your shoes, pedals, and helmet in your carry-on baggage. If your luggage is lost, it's easier to find a bike to borrow if you have your own pedals and shoes.

There are definitely significant psychological advantages to establishing a consistent pre-race routine. The pattern has a leveling effect on the stress associated with the magnitude of an event. By going through the same series of tasks as before every other race, you can make a highly stressful event as manageable as every other race. Events like national championships, world championships and the Olympics are major competitions, but you must treat the day of the event as just another race day. There should be no difference between what you do the day of the Olympic road race and what you do the day of the district championship.

No Nervous Nellies

Mike Neel, my coach during my racing career, told me once that horse trainers kick nervous people out of the stables before races. The horses sense that nervousness and become upset themselves. When I worked with the U.S. national team, I was very conscious of how I carried myself. Athletes pick up on the attitude and demeanor of their coach. I was careful to project a calm and confident demeanor during major events so as not to add to the stress the athletes already felt. When things are not going perfectly according to plan, athletes need assurance that everything is under control. A panicking coach is the last thing they need.

Confidence is infectious. A coach's confidence helps dispel the lingering doubts and fears athletes may have about their abilities. This attitude is most critical with younger or less accomplished athletes. The confident personas of champion athletes develop along with their athletic abilities.

Avoiding Micromanagement

At an event, a coach functions primarily as a director; there is very little coaching to be done. The main objective is to have an overall view of the entire event, while the athlete concentrates on smaller details. Changes in the race schedule, staging positions, and start orders are some of the matters that coaches should be on top of. They should have a rule book in the event of protests or disputes. It is generally better for a coach to deal with these issues, because the athlete is too likely to lose composure. Good officials tend to respond to sound reasoning and a little respect. Telling an official what you think of his mother is a guaranteed way to lose a protest.

A coach's most important role on race day is to be an athlete's most ardent supporter. I am always disappointed when I see coaches berating or belittling athletes. The first rule of medicine is "Do no harm." The same rule applies to coaching. Every part of a coach's relationship with athletes should help them move forward, not back. Athletes can be so hard on themselves that they need positive support to balance their self-criticism. That holds across the board—from Little League coaches to Olympic coaches.

CHAPTER 8

PREPARING FOR PARIS

CHRIS CARMICHAEL

L ance Armstrong dominated the 1999 Tour de France.* He was a confident and mature team leader in an event that demands the full capacity of its winner's abilities. Lance's victory was a story of a man's comeback from cancer to the pinnacle of sport, but it also was a story ten years in the making. His victory was the culmination of the work he began at age 18 with the U.S. National Team, nurtured under his Motorola team director and friend, Jim Ochowicz, and continued with Johan Bruyneel and Lance's outstanding teammates of the U.S. Postal Service Cycling Team. I am proud of Lance and all his achievements. He has worked hard for all he has enjoyed, and it was a pleasure to play a role in his victory in the world's greatest sporting event.

Lance Armstrong's preparation for the 1999 Tour de France began just after the 1998 Vuelta de Espana. His hard-fought fourth-place finish in the tough three-week stage race made it clear that Lance had the capability to be a Tour de France contender.

Our first step was to set up a periodization plan designed for him to reach peak fitness at the beginning of July. The idea of periodization is to break the

* This article first appeared in slightly different form in the *VeloNews 2000 Tour de France Official Guide.*

year into distinct training periods, each of which adds to the cumulative physical and mental development necessary for optimal athletic performance. At Carmichael Training Systems (CTS), we divide the training year into smaller periods of training, alternating sessions of heavy training load with recovery sessions of lower intensity or volume. Periodization involves manipulating these and other training components over the course of a week, month, year, or even longer. We break the year into four main periods: foundation, preparation, specialization, and transition. I applied these periods to Lance's training program in order to place his fitness at its optimum in July 1999.

An important factor I learned from working with Lance in 1998 was that he has a seven-week window of optimum performance. During this time, he can stay intensely focused, enabling him to make the sacrifices necessary to perform at his best. This focus helps him adhere to a strict diet and sleep regimen, which is as important to success as the workouts themselves. I designed his periodization program to place the Tour within his optimal performance window.

Lance's foundation period focused on building strength and working on pedaling mechanics. CTS developed a proprietary resistance training program that incorporates strength training off the bike and specific on-the-bike resistance training. The CTS resistance program concentrates on building strength first, leading to power later. Strength is your muscles' ability to generate force. This individually tailored resistance program focuses on an initial conditioning phase, followed by developing muscular strength by working out with heavy weights, doing low repetitions and numerous sets.

It is wonderful to be strong, but strength is useless if it cannot be applied. A unique feature of the CTS program is that it incorporates on-the-bike resistance training in order to transfer the athlete's strength gains from the gym to the pedals. Power is the application of force through a certain distance or time. Using specific workouts, Lance was able to increase the amount of power he could apply to the pedals. At this point, though, he wasn't spending much time on his bike because weight training and cycling don't mix well. In order to increase one, you need to decrease the other. It was important, then, to design rides that would provide the most benefit in the least time. Lance spent time riding a fixed-gear bike, since the low gearing and continual pedaling translate to high heart rates, increased ventilation, and good aerobic conditioning. Even though we were working on developing strength and power, aerobic conditioning was still the most important aspect of Lance's training.

Sustainable power requires a strong aerobic engine for fuel. Long road races and stage races require a large cumulative power output. Riding at higher cadences requires greater aerobic output but less power is used per pedal stroke. We knew that if Lance could generate a great deal of power while still remaining aerobic, he could meet the demands of a three-week race like the Tour de France.

In early spring , Lance moved into the preparation period of his training. Training in California and Europe, he worked to further increase his aerobic capacity with threshold workouts, lots of climbing, and some racing. Lance concentrated on racing more stage races than one-day Classics to develop his stage-race stamina as well as his mental preparedness for stage racing. He was racing for fitness during his early-season events in Europe. During this time, Lance was still working on maintaining a high cadence during both races and training. It took some time for him to get used to pedaling faster in races. Lance increased his cadence about 10–15 rpm from 80 rpm to 90+ in time trials and from 70 rpm to 80–85 while climbing. This enabled him to stay seated longer during climbs, preserving energy normally wasted by climbing out of the saddle.

At the end of the preparation period, Lance performed a CTS Field Test as a practical means of assessing his progress. The test was just one of a series of tests performed under similar conditions on the same course. The field test established Lance's maximum sustainable power output and was instrumental in refining his training intensities. As his conditioning and power progressed, it was imperative to keep his training intensities appropriate to his stage of development. After his test in the beginning of April, I was confident that he was coming into good form. Two weeks later he finished second in the Amstel Gold race.

During the specialization period, Lance started to prepare specifically for the Tour de France. While continuing to work on his aerobic capacity and pedaling style, Lance undertook two training camps in France. The training camps in the Alps and Pyrenees served two purposes: to scout the climbs and road conditions of the Tour routes and to enable Lance to visualize himself in the Tour de France and gain confidence as a result. One day in the Alps concluded with the climb up Alpe d'Huez. I was able to gather significant data on Lance from the seven-hour, cold, rainy ride, including his power outputs at the end of such a long day. Also during this specialization period, Lance began the process of leaning down for the Tour.

As the final step in his preparation, Lance's training shifted from developing energy systems to meeting racing demands. His physical preparation consisted of a series of stage races, including the Dauphine-Liberie and the Route du

Sud, while mentally he continued to focus completely on the Tour de France. Lance's life resembled that of a monk. He was devoting long hours to his passion, going to sleep at eight or nine in the evening, and eating only enough food to exceed his caloric output slightly.

At the end of June, just five days before the start of the Tour, Lance performed another CTS Field Test. I saw significant progress in his maximum sustainable power output; in fact, it was the highest I had ever seen it. That number divided by Lance's weight gave me a value in watts/kilogram, which is a critical factor for a Tour de France contender. As this value increases, so does climbing ability. I realized that Lance was in the best condition of his life. His mental awareness and focus were the strongest and tightest I had ever seen them. I knew that this Tour was going to be a historic race for American cycling.

Matt DeCanio leads the charge at the 2001 Redlands Classic. Consistency has been key to Matt's rise from a Junior National Champion to an elite professional.

CHAPTER 9

FOCUSING ON SUCCESS

KRISTEN DIEFFENBACH

I don't fail to finish because I'm physically not up to it,

but because I get mentally tired.

—MARIO CIPOLLINI, Italian cycling pro

Often the ability to stay mentally focused and strong is the biggest difference between a rider's performance success and disappointment.* Similarly, mental factors are often what separate winners from those at the back of the pack when riders of comparable physical and technical abilities compete. Athletes spend a great deal of energy and time on their physical development and the condition of their equipment; however, they frequently neglect the mental side of training and racing.

Chris Carmichael likes to tell the story of his first race as a child: After riding well, Carmichael backed off during the final rush to the finish line. A man who would become his first coach told a discouraged Carmichael, "You can't win if you don't sprint." Although the cardiovascular endurance-oriented nature of cycling demands that successful riders learn how to maintain a positive focus

This article first appeared in slightly different form in *VeloNews* 30, no. 12 (2001).

in the face of physical discomfort and fatigue, the natural tendency for many cyclists is to have negative words such as "awful," "terrible," or "toast" pop into their thoughts when their legs begin to burn or when their lungs feel as if they're about to explode. A negative mental assessment of what you're feeling, or of your ability, during a race will defeat even the strongest rider. While almost no one looks forward to pain or fatigue during a training ride or a race, successful athletes learn to deal with these distractions and are able to refocus their energy in a positive and productive way.

Several studies by sport psychology researchers John Partington, Terry Orlick, and Dan Gould have examined the psychological abilities of Canadian and American Olympic athletes. These studies found that through planned, deliberate practice many successful athletes have developed good concentration skills and are, in effect, able to redirect negative thoughts using positive, constructive self-talk. It is important to note that these mental skills rarely come naturally, but instead take the same commitment to practice as physical skills.

Contrary to what many people believe, strong mental skills, like strong physical skills, can be learned. Creating the mental skills needed to enhance focus, maintain a positive mindset, and strengthen concentration must be just as systematic and planned as the other training aspects of your cycling program. Initially the use of mental skills such as "thought-stopping," "negative-thought-countering," "personal-positives," and "cue words" should be done during routine, but nonstressful, training situations (preseason long rides on Sundays and spin rides on Friday afternoons). Concentrate on incorporating these skills into your ride before you are fatigued and using them with conscious effort. As the various techniques become a natural part of your training, focus on applying your skills in more stressful training situations when you are fatigued and during more rigorous workout efforts, such as HillClimbing repeats. Ultimately, challenge yourself to use your enhanced concentration and refocusing skills to push yourself in training and eventually in competition.

Assess Your Mental State

Before you begin working on improving your mental abilities, you must carefully assess your training and racing mindset. Take time to evaluate your concentration, focus, and internal dialogue in both practice and competitive situations. An honest self-assessment allows you to identify areas for improvement. Enlist the help of coaches, teammates, and other trusted riders to examine your strengths as well as potential areas to work on. Identify when you have the most difficulty maintaining your focus and concentration during rides and races. What factors contribute to an unfocused ride or race? When do you find yourself being negative? Targeting potential problems will help you design training situations that allow you to build the skills you need.

In addition to identifying situations where poor concentration and negative thoughts are problematic, it is important to consider the specific thoughts that undermine your riding confidence and distract you from the task at hand. Write down the negative things you say to yourself when you are tired, hurting, or discouraged, then review your list and write a positive counterstatement for each negative one. For example, counter the negative statement "This hurts so much!" with "I'm strong enough to ride through this." Look for optimistic ways to rephrase each discouraging comment, ensuring the replacement phrase or statement is positive, constructive, and something you believe. If the statement isn't something you would say to a teammate it shouldn't be something you would say to yourself.

Counter Negative Thinking

During training rides, practice identifying your negative thoughts as soon as they occur. Catching negative thoughts immediately is the first step to successfully countering them. Once a negative thought has occurred, stop it quickly by saying "stop" out loud and imagining a stop sign. Immediately replace the negative thought with one of the positive counterstatements you have created. At first this thought process may feel awkward and drawn out, but with practice it becomes more automatic. Eventually, you will be able stop negative thoughts faster, before they have a chance to become discouraging or distracting.

Positive self-talk statements can also be instrumental in enhancing focus and motivation. Recall compliments you have received from other riders and review your best training rides and races. Use these images and memories to create a list of personal-positives—phrases that bolster your belief in yourself and your abilities. Make the statements short and direct. Personal-positives can include phrases such as "It's all me," "Feel the power," "I am a great hill rider," and "I am strong." Post these statements where you can review them often, such as on the bathroom mirror, and repeat them to yourself when you train and race.

The Magic Word

The use of cue words can be a powerful technique for enhancing concentration and focus during a hard workout, a breakaway attempt, or similar situations where a powerful sustained effort is needed. Choose a cue word or sound that you associate with power and speed ("push," "boom," "power," or "go"). During training repeat your word or sound and see it in your mind as you increase your effort. Using your cue word in association with sprint and interval efforts will create a connection between your mental effort and the physical push.

In addition to using cue words and personal-positives as performance-enhancing thoughts, you can also write them out and tape them to your headset, the back of your glove, or on your handlebars. Incorporate your personal power words into your bike "mojo." This can provide a critical visual reminder when you need it most. A list of personal-positives and positive counterstatements should also be placed in your travel bag so you can review them prior to each race.

Lastly, it is important to remember that just like physical skills, your mental skills must be consciously incorporated into training over time in order to properly develop them. Furthermore, you must practice these skills regularly in order to keep them strong. Initially this will require a conscious, determined effort to ensure your focus and concentration matches your physical input, but with persistence your efforts will pay off in increased enjoyment as well as enhanced personal success.

PART TWO

TECHNIQUE

Photo by Casey B. Gibson

At the 2000 Olympic games, Marty Nothstein solidified himself as one of the premier sprinters of his generation. His gold-medal ride in the match sprint demonstrated the value of a well-balanced training program.

INTRODUCTION TO TECHNIQUE

CRAIG GRIFFIN

D uring my years with USA Cycling, I was responsible for preparing athletes for some major international competitions, including several Pan-American games, world championships, and Olympics games. The pressure on athletes at the elite level is immense. The athletes put enormous pressure on themselves, and they feel even more pressure because they are representing their country in international competition. It is unrealistic to tell athletes to approach the Olympic games as just another race; you must teach athletes to embrace the challenge of performing on the world stage. At the same time, the best way for athletes to succeed at the international level is to use the same techniques and strategies that worked to reach that level. The message to athletes is straightforward: Go out and do what you already know how to do, the things you have practiced and perfected.

In 1994, the U.S. Men's Endurance Track Team was flying. The team pursuit squad performed consistently every time they hit the track. As our plane landed in Palermo, Italy, the goal of winning America's first Team Pursuit World Championship medal seemed increasingly realistic. Riding times for the team put it in the hunt for medals along with the Germans and Australians. Everything was coming together as planned.

The Australians were the reigning world champions and world record holders, and their qualifying time proved they were the fastest team: They qualified almost six seconds faster than any other team in an event usually decided by less than two seconds. The U.S. team qualified third, which confirmed that we were a medal contender but still far off the Australians. Following a quarterfinal win over Italy, we were paired against the Australians in the semifinals. The winner would go on to compete for the world championship; the loser could do no better than a bronze medal.

The U.S. team had a mixture of experience and youth, but not a single rider on the squad had ever been in a position to medal in a world championship event. It was uncharted territory for the coaches too; none of us from USA Cycling had much experience in the medal rounds. But we had done our homework and come to Palermo prepared. The team had trained in climate-controlled rooms in Colorado Springs that were set up to simulate the temperature and humidity of Palermo. They had trained with power meters, video analysis, and the most advanced technology available. Most important, though, they had put in the necessary hours on the bike and the track.

Our strategy for facing the Australians was simple — to hit the track and do what we already knew how to do. We were going to ride the best 4,000 meters we could, because even though the Australians were superior on paper, we wanted to be prepared in case they faltered. As coaches, we made sure the athletes saw this race as an opportunity to seize, not as an insurmountable obstacle.

We stuck to a tried-and-true plan, but the Australians played around with their strategy. They changed their lineup and their timing schedule because they were looking ahead to the final instead of concentrating on the semifinal. Their normal strategy was to start fast off the start line, which they could do better than anyone else, and then ride at full throttle for the entire race. They raced the team pursuit aggressively because they had the power and speed to support their tactics. As expected, they had a great start and first kilometer, but then they backed off. They underestimated our team and figured they could save themselves for the final by soft-pedaling through our race.

The race came down the last lap. The Australians had a two-second lead over us (quite significant in a team pursuit) when they decided to save themselves for the final, but we stuck to our schedule. We closed the gap and were essentially neck and neck with 500 meters to go. The Australians tried to speed up again, but it was too late. The change they made in their lineup had reduced their overall power, and they couldn't accelerate quickly enough to match the speed we were holding. Coming across the finish line, the U.S. cyclists didn't win by much — two one-thousandths of a second (about six inches) — but for the first time in history, a team from the United States was headed to the final to race for the Team Pursuit World Championship.

If the Australians had raced that semifinal the same way they raced every other race, we couldn't have beaten them. They were a faster team. Because they deviated from the plan that had worked, we were given a window of opportunity. We beat the Australians that day because the team was prepared to seize that opportunity. They handled the pressure of the world championships by keeping things simple and relying on the skills and techniques they developed in training.

It is not necessary to change what you do in competition just because one event is bigger than another. Spend your training time learning how to perform so that when you go to an important event, you simply do what you already know how to do.

CTS member Conrad Stoltz during the running leg of the 2001 Boulder Peak Triathlon.

CHAPTER 10

RUN LIKE A GAZELLE

SCOTT SCHNITZSPAHN

In almost every sport, the athlete begins with a foundation of proper technique, then continues to build on that knowledge, always concentrating on improving his or her form.* Swimmers are taught proper stroke mechanics and body position, tennis players learn the correct way to hold a racket, and golfers are coached on the importance of follow-through. Before Little Leaguers ever take a swing, they are taught how to hold the bat. And then there is running.

Most of us begin running naturally as children at play. No coach or parent tells us how; we just run. Our parents help us take our first steps, but they figure we can handle it from there. A few of us participate in track in school and may be lucky enough to have a coach give us a few pointers. However, when most of us decide to run for competition, for recreation, or simply for exercise, we head to the local sporting goods store, try on a few pairs of shoes with colors we like, walk around the store for a few minutes to make sure they feel good, then go running. Just like that, we think we know how to run. Go to your local 5-kilometer run and you'll see that, on the whole, we have no idea what we are doing.

---

* This article first appeared in slightly different form in the August 2000 issue of *Inside Triathlon*.

The running-shoe industry has tried to teach us how to run and make it easier for us with the latest and greatest in shoe technology. Manufacturers build almost all their shoes with large heel cushions and extra rubber sole on the heel for durability. This design tells us that the proper way to run must involve striking heavily on the heel. Then, as we run more and develop nagging injuries, we deduce we must have a motion-control problem that causes foot, knee, or hip pain. Sure enough, the shoe companies have a higher-priced model with fancy motion-control devices that will cure what must be our genetic biomechanical deficiency. If the top-of-the-line shoe is not enough to solve our injury problems, perhaps a podiatrist can make us an even more expensive orthotic device that will set us straight and help us run better.

Once we've found the perfect shoe, the manufacturer inevitably discontinues that model and makes us start all over. Until then, we decide that we need to run more to get faster. We fill our training logs with big numbers. With more running, we attain higher levels of fitness, and we do get faster to a point. Eventually, we learn through coaching or magazine articles that speed work (fast running for short intervals) is the magic bullet to achieving our new personal record. But, after excessive time at the track, running until we want to throw up, we just can't get any faster. Or can we?

The most expensive shoes and all the miles and speed work in the world will not make you as fast as you could be unless you run with good technique. Yes, there is such a thing as learning how to run. And no matter how long you've been a runner, you can still change your technique. Some of us were born with good technique. Just as in other sports, there are people who are "naturals." You've seen these gazelles who seem to glide across the ground while the rest of us pound our bodies into the pavement on each stride, only to push off and do it again, step after step. If you are already a gazelle, a natural-born runner, you can stop reading this chapter now. For the rest of us, there are ways to run faster and have fewer injuries.

Warning! The running techniques described in the following paragraphs are a radical change from traditional heel-striking techniques. These technique modifications will make you a faster and more efficient runner. However, implement these changes gradually to allow the body to adapt to the new muscle and tendon movement patterns and strength needs. Like any new stress to the body, too much too fast can lead to injury. Work on each of the following running-form changes one at a time until you have mastered each one individually.

1. *Get off your heels.* Your foot should land directly underneath you as you run, and your contact point with the ground should be just behind the ball of your foot. The heel of your shoe may touch the ground slightly, but the heel of your foot should not impact the ground. Striking mid-foot directly under your center of mass eliminates the deceleration caused by heel-striking in front of your center of mass. This technique also shortens your range of motion, reducing your energy expenditure.

2. *Run on hot coals.* Shorten your impact time with the ground by pretending to run on hot coals in bare feet. The less time your foot is on the ground, the less energy is absorbed by the ground. This also shortens your range of motion by reducing the distance that your leg trails behind you while still on the ground. Again, a smaller range of motion decreases your energy output at all running speeds.

3. *Move in a straight line.* Work to minimize lateral movement of the arms and legs, particularly elbows and ankles that tend to wander away from the body, especially as fatigue sets in.

4. *Use gravity.* Run with a slightly forward total body lean. However, do not lean forward by bending at the waist. Run as if you are being pulled along by a string from your belly button. Also, do not extend your legs into the ground, but relax them and let gravity bring your foot to the ground beneath you. Natural runners make it look easy because they use gravity to their advantage.

Once you have mastered these four techniques, you will notice that your stride is shorter and that you run with less effort at the same speeds. You will know you have become a more gazelle-like runner by your quieter stride and improved stability with less unnecessary vertical and lateral movement. To track your progress over time and better identify the weak spots in your technique, have your running form videotaped at a track or treadmill. Ideally, locate an experienced coach in your area who can assess your technique and work with you to perfect your form. Some gazelles are born, but the rest of them can be built.

CHAPTER 11

SPIN DOCTOR
Why Triathletes Should Learn to Spin

CHRIS CARMICHAEL

A t the local group ride, triathletes are usually easy to spot in the pack.* They may try to hide by riding their road bikes without aerobars, but their pedal stroke will usually reveal their true identity. Many triathletes are "mashers"—their legs go up and down on the pedals with a slower cadence (70–80 revolutions per minute), and they ride in the toughest gear they can manage. Compare the masher style of pedaling to a "spinner." An experienced cyclist's legs appear to pedal in perfect circles at a higher cadence (95–110 rpm) in an easier gear. Yet the spinner maintains the same speed as the masher.

The main advantage to an efficient technique and high pedal cadence is the ability to change speeds quickly in order to respond to a sprint or other acceleration that may occur in the pack. A higher cadence and smooth stroke also allow the cyclist to ride longer at a higher speed with less muscle fatigue.

Maintaining a certain speed on a bicycle requires a specific power output to the pedals. Pedaling at a lower cadence means the rider's muscles must generate more force per pedal revolution to maintain the specific power output than if the rider were pedaling at a higher cadence. To understand this better, imagine lifting

* This article first appeared in slightly different form in the May 2000 issue of *Inside Triathlon*.

100 pounds twice versus 20 pounds 10 times. Performance will suffer if the athlete exhausts the muscles too early by exerting too much force per pedal revolution.

Lance Armstrong proved the effectiveness of a high cadence during the 35.3-mile time trial in the 1999 Tour de France. Lance won the stage by a whopping 58 seconds and maintained an average speed of over 30 mph. Whereas most riders in the Tour favored the traditional hard gear-low cadence (70–90 rpm) formula, Lance raised his cadence to a range of 100–115 rpm. He had found that he could maintain higher power outputs with this more rapid and efficient cadence. His victory in that eighth stage gave him the lead that he took all the way to Paris.

However, when I started working with Lance, he too was a masher. Tests done at the Olympic Training Center in Colorado Springs early in Lance's career revealed that he generated very little power across the top and bottom of his pedal stroke. Lance spent many years perfecting his pedal mechanics through drills and improving his cardiovascular ability to handle the higher cadences.

A higher cadence also will help a triathlete run better coming off the bike leg of a triathlon. Most elite runners, who are also very efficient in their technique, run with a foot-strike cadence of 85–90 strikes per minute per leg. Cycling with a cadence near 90 rpm, instead of the traditional 70–80 rpm that most triathletes favor, will ease the transition from bike to run and allow the triathlete to run faster and more efficiently immediately off the bike.

Tips and Drills

The following tips and drills will help any cyclist improve his or her pedaling mechanics and pedal with a faster, more efficient stroke. Remember, these drills should be done year-round, as it takes years to perfect your stroke, and many riders slip into old habits as training and racing loads increase.

1. *One-leg pedaling.* This is best performed on an indoor trainer at a moderate intensity. Don't try to pedal too hard while performing this interval or injury could occur. While pedaling, visualize scraping your toes through the bottom of the pedal stroke, as if you were trying to rub mud off your shoes. Over the top of the pedal stroke, push your pedal forward just before you reach top-dead-center. Perform 30 to 60 seconds of one-leg pedaling per interval, and perform three intervals per leg before having a rest period of 5–10 minutes. This constitutes one set. Two to three sets should be sufficient for one workout.

2. *FastPedal.* On a flat section of road, choose a relatively easy gear and begin slowly picking up your pedal speed, starting at around 15–16 pedal revolutions per 10-second count; this equates to a cadence of 90–96 rpm. While staying in the saddle, increase pedal speed and try to keep your hips from rocking. Concentrate on pulling through the bottom of the pedal stroke and over the top. After two minutes, you should be maintaining 18–20 pedal revolutions per 10-second count, or a cadence of 108–120 rpm.

Start with four to six intervals of two minutes at this cadence and increase the amount of FastPedal time 10–15 seconds each week, up to 5 minutes per interval. Your heart rate will climb while performing this workout, but don't use it to judge your training intensity. The FastPedal workout should consist of riding at the prescribed training intensity; therefore, it is important that you try to ride the entire length of this workout with as few interruptions as possible.

3. *Fixed-gear riding.* Riding a fixed-gear bicycle is very helpful for improving a rider's pedal stroke. With a fixed gear, the rider cannot coast and is limited to one gear, usually a low one that requires fast pedaling downhill and a quick cadence on the flats. Generally, fixed-gear riding is more for the competitive cyclist (and popular among urban bike messengers). Spinning classes at health clubs usually feature fixed-gear bikes, too. The nature of fixed-gear riding, standard on track bikes, helps clean up pedaling mechanics by carrying the legs through the entire pedal circle. A fixed-gear bicycle helped teach Lance to keep the pedal pressure more uniform throughout the circle for a better stroke.

CYCLING FOR FASTER RUN SPLITS

PETER REID

O ver the past three years, I have been working hard on my cycling, but my cycling splits have not gotten that much faster.* All that hard work for nothing, you would think. Well, not really, because something strange happened—I got faster on the run. As I focused more on my bike training, my running off the bike began to improve. Plus, my perceived effort on the run declined, and I had the awesome feeling of running away from everybody or chasing people down in those last few kilometers. So how do you get faster on the run through bike training?

You should think of triathlon as one sport—not three. Train as a triathlete—not as a swimmer, cyclist, and runner. I believe there are three key components to cycling training that help triathletes improve the run: bike setup, cycling efficiency, and cycling endurance.

The Setup

When setting up a triathlon race bike, you need to be aerodynamic to cut through the wind, but it is also important to be comfortable. Consider the width of the

* This article first appeared in slightly different form in the October 2001 issue of *Inside Triathlon*.

aero bar pads. Narrow pads will make you sleek, but they will also restrict breathing. If you are tight in the chest area, you will need to work harder to keep moving forward.

The second, and perhaps most important aspect of fit, is saddle height. If my saddle is off a few millimeters, I feel it. The most common problem with saddle height is that people are riding too high. If your leg becomes straight while you are pedaling, the saddle is much too high. A good indicator is to have someone ride behind you to see if your hips are rocking from side to side. If they are, the saddle is too high. Work in small increments when adjusting saddle height, because just a few millimeters will make a big difference. The goal is to achieve a fluid pedal stroke without any upper-body movement—your legs should be the only things that move. If the upper body is moving, you're wasting energy that will be needed for the run. The goal is to set up the bike so that you are comfortable and efficient.

Think Efficiency

Now that your upper body is set, you need to focus on cycling efficiency. Cycling efficiency refers to the amount of energy required to move the bike forward. An inefficient pedal stroke will make you push against yourself rather than let you drive all the energy into the gears. My biggest problem for years was that my downstroke was fighting the upstroke every time I turned the pedals. For instance, as I was pushing down with my right leg, part of the energy was going into lifting my left leg instead of moving the bike forward. Studies have shown that no additional power is generated in the upstroke, but it is possible to unweight the pedal as it rises, thus reducing the resistance against the opposite leg.

When I begin my rides, I try to focus on working the upstrokes so that I get the feeling of releasing pressure on the pedals during the upstroke phase of the pedal stroke. A great tool for cycling efficiency is the Spin Scan on CompuTrainers. The Spin Scan shows what each leg is doing during the pedal stroke—you can see if you are pushing against yourself instead of driving the gears.

The second aspect to improve is pedaling cadence. Too many triathletes mash the gears. Pushing a big gear takes a huge amount of muscle strength but does not translate into huge power. Just recall Lance Armstrong in the Tour de France the past three years. His cadence was higher than that of most of the other riders—and he was going faster than the rest of the peloton. A higher cadence taxes the aerobic system more than a lower cadence, but it requires less muscle strength—strength that you can save for the run. Mashers tend to ride fast but go on to slow run splits because their muscles are fatigued.

Building Endurance

The next process is cycling endurance, which involves long, steady miles in the saddle. If you are getting ready for an Ironman, you need to do a few rides of at least four to five hours. Some of these rides should be done solo. Why solo? It builds mental strength—endurance of the mind. If you ride with a group, how much time are you in front blocking the wind for the rest of the group? You are probably in the lead less than 75 percent of the time. I consider a six-hour group ride about equal to a four-hour solo ride. Plus, when you are with a group, you have other people to motivate you. Going solo forces you to push yourself.

I believe the long ride is more about mental training than physical training. Sure, the more miles you put on the bike, the more efficient you will become with your pedal stroke and aerobic system—this translates into more energy for the run. But there are so many times during the run that the mind wanders and loses focus. The more you adapt to pushing yourself, the easier it will be on race day.

The goal is to start the run section strong and fresh. To do this, you must focus a bit more on the bike. Remember, you are a triathlete, and you need to train as a triathlete.

CHAPTER 13

TACTICS FOR DRAFT-LEGAL RACING

CHRIS CARMICHAEL

The cycling leg of a triathlon has traditionally been considered an individual time trial with athletes riding as fast as possible with the aid of only their aerodynamic equipment.* Drafting during the cycling leg was punishable by time penalties and disqualification. However, in recent years, draft-legal triathlons have changed the demands of the cycling leg.

Successful Olympic-distance triathletes in this style of racing need to add cycling skill and tactical development to their event preparation. Even if you don't race draft-legal triathlons, or if you're among the folks who feel that drafting undermines the integrity of what is supposed to be an individual sport, knowing how to draft effectively can still be a useful skill. In training, effective pacelining can make a ride safer and more efficient and make you look like a tri-star on your local club rides. Also, if you ever decide to jump into a cycling race for some early-season speed training, knowing what you're doing will help prevent you from standing out as the token tri-geek in the peloton.

---

* This article first appeared in slightly different form in the June 2001 issue of *Inside Triathlon*.

Drafting

Drafting is nothing new to endurance sports. Cyclists, distance runners, and car racers have used the benefits of drafting for years. Many people debate the merits of wheelsucking in triathlon, but the fact is that the merits of drafting are well established.

Drafting is so effective because a cyclist riding in another rider's slipstream expends up to 30 percent less energy than the cyclist plowing through the wind. This fact is used to everyone's advantage when riders work together in pacelines in order to share the work. A pack of cyclists in a rotating paceline can travel much faster than any one of those cyclists alone. The critical consideration in drafting is finding the slipstream and staying in it. Conventional wisdom holds that riding directly behind another rider will put you in that rider's slipstream, and sometimes that may be the case—when there is little or no wind, or the wind is coming from directly in front or behind you. However, considering the 360 degrees of possibility and, of course, Murphy's Law, drafting is rarely so straightforward.

When the wind is coming from the side, it is more effective to move from directly behind a rider to partially beside him or her. For instance, when the wind is blowing in from the right, it would be best to move to the left of the rear wheel of the rider ahead of you. As the severity of a cross-wind increases, you will need to move forward so that your shoulder pulls even with the leading rider's hip. Several riders drafting in this manner give the paceline the shape of a wedge, a formation known as an echelon.

The challenge of an echelon is that only so many riders can fit in the width of a lane. If 10 riders can position themselves in the echelon, the 11th rider is at the edge of the road, unable to move to the appropriate side of the preceding rider. This rider is out of the draft and at a serious disadvantage.

Take a cue from professional cyclists and form a second echelon instead of wasting your energy fighting in the gutter for a draft that will never materialize. In windy conditions, it is important to be in the front echelon group because it will most likely consist of the strongest riders and leave the other echelons behind.

If the wind is coming from the right, the lead rider of the echelon would be on the far right side of the road, and the wedge would extend back over his left shoulder. To rotate through an echelon, the rider at the front of the wedge-shaped formation drops back as the next rider moves forward and to the right to take the lead. The rider dropping back will start moving left toward the trailing edge of the echelon. Since riders should spend only a short time exposed to the wind at the head of an echelon, there is a nearly constant rotation. The pulling line moves right and the recovering line moves left behind it. The direction of rotation is reversed when the wind is coming from the left. Riding in an echelon is an advanced skill and should be practiced to ensure safety. Also, if you're on an open road, pay attention for vehicle traffic — never attempt this maneuver if there are cars behind you or oncoming.

Breakaways

Although drafting in a pack or paceline conserves energy, it also means starting the run leg with a potentially large group of competitors. That raises the concept of breaking away. Leaving the other athletes behind and arriving in T2 (transition from bike to run) with a large lead can be beneficial, sometimes: Even in a nondrafting event, dropping a group of riders before T2 will allow you more elbow room and will give you a cushion starting the run.

Drafting or nondrafting, you must balance the potential time gain with the energy cost of riding faster than a group of cyclists. In short triathlons, the cycling leg is too brief to gain a sizable lead in a breakaway. In general, if the cycling leg is 12 kilometers or less, a breakaway is unlikely to gain you enough of a gap to be worth the energy cost.

A breakaway of three or more riders has a considerably higher chance of success than a solo rider does. But if you do the lion's share of the work, you are burning more energy than your breakaway companions, and that will hurt you in the run. Refusing to do your fair share of the work isn't a good idea either, as it leads to a smaller time gap coming into T2. When breakaway riders don't cooperate well, they also run the risk of getting caught by the main peloton, in which case each breakaway rider's energy has been wasted.

Attacking

So, you've looked at the course and the riders in the group, and you have decided that a breakaway is a good idea. Now what? The first kilometer of a breakaway is the hardest and most critical. Your initial acceleration should be very hard so that a gap opens quickly. If your acceleration is too soft, the whole group lines up in your draft and you just wasted a big chunk of energy. Depending on your personal strengths, you can use the course to your advantage. Successful attacks often go on climbs or through technical sections.

Once you have a small gap, you have to pour on the power to make it grow quickly. You want to create a sizable gap so that the other riders have to consider the energy cost of bridging to you. If everyone waits for someone else to commit, you're away. Once your lead is established, settle into the maximum intensity you can sustain, and turn your focus to what's ahead rather than who's behind you.

Bridging

When someone else instigates an attack, you have very little time to consider your options. The longer you wait, the more energy it will take to bridge the gap. Try to evaluate who is in the attack: 1. Are they capable of riding away? 2. Is the group you are in capable of catching them? If you answer yes to 1 and no to 2, then it's time to go for a bridge.

The thing to remember about bridging to a breakaway is that you are trying to join the breakaway, not bring the whole group up to it. This means that if you can't go with the initial attack, you may be better off waiting until the attack gets clear of the peloton. It becomes a balancing act. If the gap is not established yet, you may inadvertently fill it, allowing the peloton to use you to maintain contact with the fledgling breakaway. If you wait too long, it will take a lot of energy to bridge the gap, and you run the risk of stalling somewhere in the no-man's-land between the breakaway and the peloton.

The effort to bridge to a breakaway starts with the same kind of attack that started the break in the first place. A 5- to 15-second lead is sufficient for you to create a gap between you and the peloton before you reach the break-away. It is also small enough for you to have the energy to keep up with the breakaway once you get there. If you end up stranded in no-man's land and the peloton is close behind you, it is smart to let them catch you so that you can get back in the draft, recover, and maybe try again.

What About the Run?

It would be wise to consider the demands of the running leg when making tactical decisions in the cycling leg. From an energy-conservation standpoint, riding with a large pack is best, but there is a higher risk of crashing, and you start the run with a large group. Triathletes who excel in the run may benefit from staying in the large group because they will be fresher for their strongest leg of the race. Strong cyclists can level the playing field by using tactical cycling to make the stronger runners burn more energy before the run. Consider your strengths to determine what you need to do in order to reach T2 prepared to have a great run.

CHAPTER 14

GET DOWN, GET DOWN

JESS SWIGGERS

I love going downhill on a mountain bike; it makes up for all that time going uphill.* But becoming a good descender takes training—with or without downhill bikes and body armor. No problem. Downhill training is fun, and in no time at all it can elevate you from a middle-of-the-pack sport racer to the expert level.

Gaining between 30 seconds and several minutes on a descent is a very real possibility, and gaining time on the downhills is easier than on the climbs because it's about gaining skill, not fitness. In any race between riders of equal fitness, the better descender will win. And that better descender will use less energy than someone who's bouncing all over the trail. Scott Moninger won the 2000 Red Zinger Classic by using a mountain bike on the descents; he didn't necessarily go faster than I did, but using a mountain bike allowed him to save valuable energy for the last two climbs.

So how do you train to go downhill faster? It requires more than just riding a bunch of descents, although that can't hurt. Just as with other aspects of racing, you have to identify your weaknesses and train them. I've always been a good

* This article first appeared in slightly different form in *VeloNews* 29, no. 17 (2000).

descender, but early on I noticed I was much better at turning to my left than to my right. I don't know why, but that wasn't the point. What mattered was fixing the problem, so I practiced right-hand turns on a dirt road until I was comfortable with them. I also discovered some general strategies for improving descending skills, which you can follow:

1. *Cut your turns.* It's best to practice this on a dirt road, preferably one with a slight grade and no traffic. Start riding and turning back and forth, as if you're slaloming the turns. With each turn, slightly increase your speed and cut the turn a bit sharper. This way you get the feel of where the breaking point is for traction. For me, knowing that point helps my confidence, and I can really start to push the limit and slide a little, all the while staying in control. It helps to do this with flat pedals, sometimes with both feet on the pedals and sometimes with your inside foot off the pedal. When your inside foot is off the pedal, it should be pointing to the inside of the turn as a stabilizer, so that you can save yourself if you lose traction completely.

2. *Start slowly and smoothly.* I often ride a little slower down the first descent of a training ride, concentrating on riding smoothly and not wasting energy. This helps me get into a rhythm, so that I can fly down the next descents with confidence. It's better to start slowly, instead of forcing the pace before you're ready. If you concentrate on picking good lines and eliminating mistakes, you'll be amazed at how fast you can go.

3. *Watch and envision.* Watching other riders is a good way to see what you should look like, and a picture in your head can help your coordination. I

watch good riders ride a section and then think about how I need to ride it. Watch great downhillers and the lead riders on any cross-country descent, and you'll learn a lot simply by observing. Also watch riders who aren't that good to help identify mistakes you need to avoid.

4. *Brake less—and sooner.* Concentrate on using your brakes less and using them before a corner rather than in it. This is good for keeping your momentum going. When I approach a corner, I brake early and try to exit with as much speed as possible. Look for a smooth arc through corners, and do the majority of your braking before the turn starts. Try not to lock the brakes or scrub more speed than you have to. Find a corner to practice in and do repeated runs, boosting the speed a bit with each run. This is a good application of the traction drill mentioned in item 1.

5. *Be a shuttle monkey.* I improved significantly by having someone shuttle me to the top of a trail, allowing me to do repeated downhill runs. I like to climb, but hitching a ride to the top means that I'm fresh for each run, not tired from riding up the hill. This frees me to concentrate more on technique; I can do climbing workouts another day. Also, riding the same trail over and over again helps you see progress: You know you're improving when you start riding the same descent faster. Shake things up sometimes by riding a trail you don't normally do (or have never done), to make sure you really are improving, and not just getting familiar with a local descent.

As you focus on your downhill skills, you'll face the fear of crashing. When you're trying to go fast, you run the risk of losing it; but if that happens, don't panic. Sometimes, reflexes and experience are the only things that get a bike pointed in the right direction again, and I can't help you with that. What I can tell you, though, is to keep your feet on the pedals — at least one foot. If both feet come out, you're probably going to crash. Hard. Use your brakes to slow down, not a tree.

When you do crash, you'll probably feel shaken up. But if you're not suffering from any major injuries, that old saying about getting back on the horse holds true. However, resist the urge to charge off at full tilt right away. Ride easy, get your confidence back, and you'll be flying again shortly. But if you can't get the crash out of your mind, there's only one thing to do: Go back to the scene of the crime and re-ride that section, just to prove to yourself that you can do it.

I definitely recommend branching out. Racing downhill is an excellent idea for cross-country riders. I raced downhill as a junior, and it boosted my descending skills tremendously. The same goes for BMX. Without suspension, your body has to soak up all the bumps, so you get a crash course on handling skills and coordination. Then there's motocross, which is particularly useful — and fun — for downhill racers. The higher speeds and more sophisticated suspension definitely translate back to the mountain bike.

As you improve your descending skills, you'll become a more complete and confident racer. Think about it: You spend time training for everything else, so why not train on fun stuff, too?

CHAPTER 15

CRITERIUM TACTICS

DEDE DEMET-BARRY

Although many North American riders excel at both criteriums and road races, the two events are very different, and each calls for its own kind of physical, mental, and tactical preparation.* Criteriums are high-speed events, generally shorter in length than long-distance road races, and not usually requiring the same climbing strength and endurance. So naturally, crits tend to favor sprinters. Even so, riders lacking the fast-twitch fibers can still stack up wins if they are good at positioning and have a high top-end speed.

Positioning is vital in criterium racing. When there are many turns, it's hard to move up. If you can get to the front and stay there, it is much easier to cover the moves, and your chances of being in the right place for the sprints are much better. It's amazing how well nonsprinters can do in criterium field sprints if they position themselves well and can corner fast.

In a criterium, a strong time trialist should always attack and try to get away. Once you are off the front, speed is the name of the game. You can gain a lot of time through the turns, which is where you must take the best line possible and pedal as fast as you can. A solo rider or a small breakaway group can go much

* This article first appeared in slightly different form in *VeloNews*.

faster through the corners than the peleton can, and there is much less chance for injury.

Because criteriums rarely exceed two hours in length, you cannot approach them as tactically as you would a road race. In a long road race, it may be possible to sit back and let other riders go up the road early, banking on the fact that they may lack the stamina to go the distance at a high speed. So professional teams will often let a break go up the road and gain minutes before they set the tempo and bring it back or make an attempt to bridge, but in criteriums this tactic is risky. If a break gets a big gap, there isn't a great deal of time to bring it back. The experienced rider tries to keep a tight grip on the race tactics to ensure that the vital moves are covered.

There are, however, a variety of successful techniques used in road racing that can be employed to win a criterium: field sprints, solo breakaways, or small group breakaways with a sprint at the end. As you train for a criterium, you should do a lot of speed work, regardless of your individual strengths. Motorpacing, sprint workouts, and short intervals will help tune up your engine. Then, in order to win crits, you must know and use your strongest attributes:

- If you are a sprinter, you must conserve your strength in the race, stay up front so that you do not miss the moves and can cover the attacks, and be sure not to waste any energy. And when it comes down to the finish, you must be able to rely upon your teammates for a lead-out. If you do not have teammates to lead you out, you must jockey for the best wheel in the pack.

- If you are a time trialist, you must take your chances before the finish. You must attack and try to get up the road.

- If endurance is your best attribute, try to get off the front early—and stay there.

Knowledge of your strengths, a lot of practice, and good technique—these are the keys to winning.

CHAPTER 16

YOU CAN'T WIN IF YOU DON'T SPRINT

CHRIS CARMICHAEL

Y ou force the breakaway on the hardest part of the course; others are coming off the back as you climb steadily and strongly.* As you crest the hill, you look around and do a quick count: Six of you are in the lead group. You're happy. Everyone is working well together, and it is clear that the breakaway is going to stick. With less than five miles to the finish line, the panic begins, and it is going to come down to a sprint. Given your history, you will undoubtedly finish last in the sprint. Your hard training is going to earn you only sixth place. The majority of the races you enter will come down to a sprint of some kind, whether it's a breakaway with a few riders or a huge field sprint. Needless to say, the ability to sprint swiftly and effectively is critical to cycling success.

Sprinting Defined

In order to improve your sprinting, you need to examine all the components that make up a successful sprint. Leg speed improves when the blueprint from the motion migrates from the cognitive brain toward the limbs. Sprinting well

* This article first appeared in slightly different form in *VeloNews* 28, no. 13 (1999).

involves constant practice, as physical and tactical elements need to be developed. Quick, speedy efforts happen with practice, practice, and more practice. Take top-end speed for example—it is a measurement of the highest speed that can be attained during a sprint. A strong top-end speed is critical in keeping opponents at bay while they try to come around you during the last few meters of a sprint.

But top-end speed does not guarantee sprinting success. Explosive power to accelerate quickly must be considered. An athlete who lacks explosive power can easily be left behind. Quickness refers to your ability to perform specific movements in the shortest possible time. It is the ability of the nervous system to process and produce rapid muscle contractions, which occur at the start of the sprint or during the accelerating phases of sprinting.

Generally, finishing sprints in the United States are shorter and require less top-end speed than those in Europe. Quickness and explosive power are the more desirable elements of U.S. sprints. The reason for this is the large number of criteriums held in the United States. The many corners preceding the finish line tend to shave off top speed, and often it is the first person out of the last corner who gets the win. This places a greater emphasis on quickness and short, explosive acceleration power.

Normally, finishing sprints with professionals in Europe are conducted at a higher maximum speed. The teams that have sprinters begin increasing speed from as far out as 20 to 30 miles. It is not uncommon that with 1 mile to go, the peleton is hitting speeds of more than 40 mph and the sprint has yet to begin.

While coaching athletes who compete in both the United States and Europe, I take into consideration the general makeup of the sprints in which they will be involved. Although the five-step model presented here is designed to improve both speed and quickness, examining the exact demands and skills needed for your races will yield greater returns.

Adding Sprints to Your Training Program

Noel Dejonckheere, the former director of the Motorola Cycling Team, likes to say that including sprints in your weekly training program will "give you a one- to two-wheel advantage at the finish line." His recommendations ring true. I often see peak-power increases with athletes who begin adding sprints to their training programs. Using power meters can give an athlete tremendous sprinting feedback. Using power to measure the intensity of each sprint has many uses. With the power meter, I no longer need to rely on the perceived intensity of the sprint to determine the total number of sprints to include in each workout. Once peak power drops off during a sprint workout, there is no need to continue.

Training with power is useful in manipulating the terrain upon which to perform the sprints. I do this with George Hincapie, who participates in the long, high-speed European sprints. Due to the increase in aerodynamic drag at higher speeds, power demands are huge. Often we will duplicate the same power demands by using a downhill road that carries Hincapie at high speeds, and as the road flattens out he begins his sprint. By leading into his sprint at more than 30 mph as he comes off the descent, he is able to sprint past 40 mph on the level road.

I suggest adding one to two sprint sessions weekly to your training program. Sprint training is not interval training; full recovery between sprints is very important. Normally, 5–20 minutes will give you enough recovery before adding another sprint to your workout. If you let your sprint go dormant, it will decline, and if you never had one, you will need to develop it for your arsenal. Here are five steps to follow for improved sprinting:

Basic Conditioning

Begin sprint training after you have a solid base of fitness and miles. You should have developed your strength, endurance, and aerobic conditioning before heading into sprint training.

Phase 1 Sprint Development

These sprints develop strength and explosive power against medium heavy to very heavy pedal resistance. It is important first to develop your functional strength and power before advancing to quicker and faster sprint workouts. Here's how to do it: (1) Slow your bike to a near stop on flat terrain while in a hard gear. (2) Next, explode out of the saddle in the same gear, pulling on the handlebars and driving the pedals down as hard as possible with each pedal stroke. You will struggle in the large gear, and the resistance will be high, but don't shift at all. Keep the sprint very short, 8–10 seconds long. (3) Give yourself 5–20 minutes recovery between the three to six total sprints. Normally, three weeks of this type of sprint training should result in more quickness and explosive sprints.

Phase 2 Sprint Development

These sprints focus on high-speed pedaling at a moderate resistance. How to do these: (1) On flat terrain, you should be rolling along at a moderate speed (18–22 mph) in a light gear; (2) jump out of the saddle, accelerating the entire time, and return to the saddle after a few seconds focusing on maintaining high pedal speed in a smooth and efficient form for the entire sprint; and (3) once you return to the saddle, shift gears as needed in order to keep accelerating.

These sprints should last 10–12 seconds and be performed once or twice during the week. Two weeks in Phase 2 will be plenty of time for proper adaptation to move on to Phase 3.

Phase 3 Sprint Development

These sprints focus on developing the same sprint intensity (I define in wattage) you face while in competition: (1) on flat terrain with a tail wind, roll up to a quick pace (22–25 mph), attack out of the saddle in large gear, but do not be overgeared; and (2) once you are back in the saddle, maintain your speed, shifting gears as necessary, and focus on keeping your speed high but floating ever so slightly during the middle portion of your sprint and kicking hard during the last 3–5 seconds of the sprint.

These sprints should be 12–15 seconds in length, with two to five total sprints per session and performed twice a week. Two weeks of Phase 3 gives you plenty of top-end sprint speed to be able to gain all that you can from Phase 4.

Phase 4 Sprint Development

This is the final step in improving sprint speed. The workout aims to improve your sprint by applying over-speed techniques, pedaling, and reaction time: (1) on a slight downhill road while at high speed (at least 25–30 mph), jump out of the saddle in a moderate gear, accelerate as hard as possible, and keep leg speed high while returning to the saddle; and (2) shift gears as needed to keep your speed accelerating for the entire downhill sprint.

These sprints should be longer in length, and you should focus on maintaining your top-end speed for the entire sprint. Do these one to two times per week with two to four sprints per session and full recovery between sprints.

• • • •

Developing your sprint is a year-round process and shouldn't be neglected. Feel free to rotate between each of these four sprint workouts. Add either more explosive power sprints or top-end speed sprints based on the current state of your sprint.

You can easily strike a balance between endurance and aerobic development and still have time to train for the high power demands of sprinting. A good example of this is the preparation Lance Armstrong did for the 1998 World Championships. The World Professional Road Championships are more than 150 miles long and require huge aerobic energy. For this, aerobic training is critical and is often the difference between winning and finishing second, separated by the smallest of margins. After the Vuelta a Espana, Lance's training program included more sprinting. He skipped the high-speed sprints and focused more on developing the shorter, lower-speed type of sprint. We assumed that a sprint at the end of the World Championships would be somewhat short and that he would have only a limited number of riders to contend with. So his sprint training needed to focus on explosive efforts starting at a relatively low speed and accelerating all the way to the finish. After integrating these sprints into his training, he gained confidence along with a higher peak power output. Lance won his group's sprint for fourth place by less than a half wheel. His sprint workouts clearly played in his favor. Dejonckheere was correct in saying that you can gain a wheel or two by training your sprint.

PART THREE

TRAINING

Matt DeCanio climbing at the head of the field at the 2001 Tour of Willamette.

INTRODUCTION TO TRAINING

JIM RUTBERG

"Chris Carmichael called. Call him back." That was the note I found upon my return from a long, cold January training ride in Winston-Salem, North Carolina. I had been training full-time and working part-time to support my habit for the better part of two years. I wanted to be an Olympian, but as I sat on the floor of a rat-hole apartment that day, eating tuna fish and beans straight out of their respective cans, my goal never seemed so far out of reach.

Chris had gotten my phone number from George Hincapie. For the past two months, I had been commuting an hour each way to train with George and a few other riders in Charlotte. One Saturday morning I asked George for some advice about coaches. I was working with a coach already, but my progress seemed to have stagnated in recent months. I asked him if he knew of any good coaches that ould work with me. He said he would be talking to his coach, Chris Carmichael, after this ride, and that he would ask Chris about it. I thanked him for his help and the ride went on.

A few hours later, the group had dwindled to just four of us, and George decided it was time to do his prescribed workout. He described it as a "medium-hard Tempo workout." The next thing I knew we were flying through the North Carolina countryside at nearly 30 miles an hour. Up hills, through corners, and over railroad tracks, the speed never let up. I rotated through the paceline once and realized that a second pull would probably lead to a long, solitary ride home. Since I had no idea where we were, getting dropped was not an option. I hung on to the back of that group for the next hour and fifteen minutes. When George signaled that his workout was over, I was still there, drooling and totally drained, but there. I found the phone message from Chris the following afternoon.

To this day I still have no idea what George said to Chris or whether the effort I put in on that Saturday had anything to do with Chris's calling me, but I would like to believe that it did. After a few days of phone tag, I was again sitting on the floor, armed with a can opener, when the phone rang. Chris told me that George had asked him to give me a call, and then he offered to be my coach. I hung up the phone and consumed the best-tasting can of beans I have ever had. My good friend and training partner, Sterling, came over to celebrate the news with me. I felt like an actor who had just gotten his big break. I'll never forget what Sterling said that day, "Well, boy, you still have a long climb ahead of you, but at least now you have a tailwind."

When I received my first month of training from Chris, I was disappointed. It was too easy. Did Chris think this was all I was capable of? I called him and explained that I could do more. He listened to me and then told me to trust him and try things his way. His way was simple and effective. The quality of my training improved, my confidence increased, and my racing results improved. I never made it to the Olympics, but I got a lot closer than I would have on my own.

In June 2000, Chris offered me a job with his new coaching company, Carmichael Training Systems. I am unique among the CTS coaching staff; I am the only one who has been on both sides of the CTS program. Athletes I work with are disappointed when they receive their first month of training. "It's too easy; I can do more than this." Trust me, I say, try things my way.

CHAPTER 17

FUNCTIONAL STRENGTH TRAINING FOR TRIATHLETES

TIM CROWLEY

The goal of this chapter is to present principles of functional strength training (FST) for optimal triathlon performance.* The methods described are designed to make you a stronger, faster, and injury-free athlete. Not only is this important for athletic performance, but also the evidence is mounting rapidly that strength training is essential for health and longevity.

Misconceptions About Strength Training

To overcome certain misconceptions about strength training, it is necessary to know some basic facts about it. Strength and size are not synonymous. The goal for triathletes when it comes to strength development is to become stronger without adding muscle bulk. Many believe strength training will slow them down. Research done on athletes at the 1970 Olympics in Mexico proved that Olympic weight lifters were faster than 100-meter sprinters in a 30-meter sprint. Other athletes claim that strength training will lead to decreased flexibility. Those same Olympic weight lifters in 1970 were the second-most flexible athletes.

* This article first appeared in slightly different form in *Inside Triathlon*.

Swimming, biking, and running are not enough to maintain strength levels. Research has revealed that beginning about the early thirties, athletes lose approximately a half pound of lean muscle per year if they do not engage in intense strength training. This loss will result regardless of their amount of aerobic activity. To maintain fast-twitch muscle-fiber strength, which is needed for sprinting and climbing, you must use in your strength sessions 75 percent of the most weight you can lift one time (1 rep max). This equates to the amount you can lift 10–12 times.

FST does not require a large time commitment. Many times, maximal gains in strength and power can be achieved in two 30- to 50-minute sessions per week, and those sessions don't have to involve going to the gym.

A year-round strength program is required. Many athletes engage only in off-season strength programs. This can lead to less than optimal strength when it counts the most. In six weeks, an athlete can lose 40 percent of strength gains if in-season strength training is not continued. After ten weeks, the same athlete may have lost up to 70 percent. In-season strength training should consist of one to two sessions per week in the gym, and another specific strength session in each of triathlon's three disciplines.

Triathlon-Specific Training

Strength training for multisport athletes has unique challenges. These athletes need to maximize strength without the risk of overtraining. The FST exercises selected for the strength program should be specific, require stabilization, be explosive/power based, and have an acceleration/deceleration component. It is important to train movements, not muscles. The exercise movements should closely resemble those of triathlon. One training component often ignored is stabilization. This is the body's ability to control movement efficiently and provide a stable platform for action of the limbs. For triathletes, this means training the stability of the lower limbs (ankle, knee, and hip), torso, and shoulders.

Another variable essential for a triathlon-specific program is power development. Strength alone will not make you powerful. Strength must be converted to power in order to be useful to triathletes. Two of the best methods of training for power are the use of explosive lifts, such as Olympic lifts, and medicine ball training. The most specific conversion sessions would involve swimming, cycling, and running against high resistance with relatively low rpms, such as cycling and running up steep grades or swimming with a drag suit or other resistance tool.

FST Characteristics

The FST method is very specific to the demands of the athletic activity. This training can include free weights, cable machines, elastic bands or tubing, stability balls, medicine balls, and balance boards. FST exercises have the following qualities:

1. Progressive: Begin with simple exercises and progress in intensity and difficulty.

2. Multiplanar: Movements are not restricted to a single direction.

3. Velocity-specific: The exercises duplicate the speed of movement required by the individual disciplines of triathlon.

4. Specificity: The movement pattern of the exercise duplicates that of swimming, cycling, and running.

5. Balance-dominated: Increases in stabilization will aid in increasing efficiency and reducing the risk of injuries.

6. Fun: If you don't enjoy the process, you won't get the most out of it.

Tools of the Trade

The equipment described here is ideally suited for FST and can be found at most good training facilities. Free weights are versatile and the equipment of choice for explosive strength training. They require a lot of stabilization and can be moved in all three planes. Explosive lifts such as Olympic lifts (clean and jerk and snatch lifts) are excellent for developing full body power and stabilization. These lifts are the cornerstone of strength training in most sports. Correct and flawless form is critical when doing Olympic lifts, and you should receive instruction and supervision from a qualified strength and conditioning coach if you choose to perform these lifts.

Stability balls have gained popularity in the past few years. These large inflatable training devices are ideal for torso training. They can also be used as an unstable bench for conventional strength exercises such as chest presses or dumbbell flys. This will increase the involvement of the shoulder stabilizers, which are vital for all swimmers.

Cables are ideal for any pulling exercise. They can be used in all directions as well as in twisting rotational exercises. Tubing with handles can do virtually everything cables can, and it is portable and comes in different thicknesses to provide variable resistance loads. Upper- and lower-body, as well as torso, exercises can be executed with both pulleys and cables.

Triathletes often neglect the musculature of the lower leg in strength training. Unfortunately, it is also the source of many overuse injuries in runners. By adding a balance board under the supporting leg for any single-leg exercise, such as a one-legged squat, you can get the muscles of the lower leg heavily involved. If the balance board is large enough, a two-legged squat can also be done effectively.

Unlike the old leather medicine balls, today's balls are made of rubber and are great for throwing drills that integrate the upper body and torso, developing power and stability. Medicine balls can be used for external resistance in stability ball exercises. They can also serve as a stability device when you are doing push-ups with a medicine ball under each hand. This turns an ordinary push-up into a very functional exercise.

Putting It into Action

This all sounds great, but where do you begin? First, make a list of the functional tools you have available to you. Next, look at your current strength program (you do have one?) and evaluate it for its functionality. The third step is to use the methods outlined here to create a more triathlon-specific routine. Often these changes result in a lowering of the weight or resistance needed to complete the exercise successfully. Begin by introducing FST into your warm-up exercises. Then integrate them into your lower intensity sets before making them the primary exercises.

8 Effective Exercises for Triathletes

Here are eight great FST exercises specific to triathletes.

1. Single-leg squat: With arms out in front, squat with one leg until knee is bent to nearly 90 degrees, then press back up to a standing position. (with or without a balance board).

2. Stability ball push-up: Feet are on the floor, and hands are on the ball.

3. Split squat: Rear foot on a 12–18 inch box, front foot 4–6 feet in front of box (balance board can be used under front foot).

4. Horizontal cable row on stability ball: While seated on the ball, pull bar attached to cable at shoulder height. Cable stays parallel to the floor. Squeeze shoulder blades together.

5. Overhead squat: Hold a barbell overhead with elbows locked and complete a squat with perfect form.

6. Single-arm dumbbell snatch: This variation of the Olympic lift will enhance full body strength and shoulder stability.

7. Single-leg cable row: Standing on the left leg, grasp a low cable with the right hand. Complete a row pulling the hand toward the shoulder while maintaining balance.

8. Curl press: With dumbbells, complete a curl movement. With hands at shoulder level, do an overhead press to complete one rep. Return to start and repeat.

Reps and Sets

How many sets and reps of each exercise are required for optimal benefit? If you are training for maximal strength, which is advisable during the foundation period of training, aim for a range of 2–3 sets of 3–8 repetitions per set.

Power training will require less weight than strength training. This allows for maximal speed of movement and high nervous-system recruitment. To avoid nervous-system fatigue, a pattern of 5–6 reps per set for 2–4 sets is recommended.

Muscle endurance requires a much higher rep range per set but fewer sets. Only 1–2 sets are needed, since the reps can be as few as 15 or as many as 100 reps per set.

FST increases your power, strength, and stability for years to come. The ideas presented here are only a sample of what is possible through FST. I recommend you find a trainer or coach versed in FST to assist you in technique. The only limits are your creativity and desire to improve as an athlete.

CHAPTER 18

HOW CAN YOU RESIST?

Resistance Training Can Be a Powerful Off-Season Tool

MIKE NIEDERPRUEM

Every off-season, cyclists of all ages, levels, and specialties consider resistance training as a way to improve on-bike strength and power.* Then, as spring approaches, many come to realize that all that work didn't enable them to meet their expectations. At the very least, hours of training time were wasted; and at the worst, days or even weeks were lost due to soreness or injury.

Does this mean that resistance training, or weight lifting, isn't applicable to a cyclist's training regimen? No. It does mean that resistance training is a "tool," and like many tools, it must be used correctly. Just because you go out to the hardware store and buy the best power tools doesn't mean you can build a house. Joining the hottest new health club and spending hours in front of the mirrors each day doesn't mean you're going to be better on the bike, but resistance training can be an effective supplement to training in the off-season.

By following a few simple guidelines, you can increase strength and power in the gym. More important, you can translate these improvements to the bike. Here's how.

* This article first appeared in slightly different form in *VeloNews*.

First, make sure your program includes "progressive overload." This means your program should periodically increase in difficulty as you adapt to the initial demands of resistance training. You will be better off in the long run by being conservative in adjusting your resistance periodically. Many athletes, especially cyclists, plateau too quickly or cause unnecessary soreness by increasing the resistance too soon and too often. A good rule of thumb is to increase your resistance only once every three or four sessions.

Second, the most effective resistance-training program is "specific" to the cyclist in question. Although a detailed plan for all disciplines is beyond the scope of the discussion here, some general characteristics are applicable to all:

- Warm up gradually (10–20 minutes of low-intensity aerobic exercise).
- Stretch before beginning your routine (and preferably, after you warm up).
- Allow 1–2 minutes of recovery between each set.
- Perform "whole body" exercises (exercises that use multiple joint movements) first.
- Perform exercises that involve large muscle masses (e.g., legs) first.
- Unless you have experience with free weights, consider weight machines as a safer alternative.
- Pay special attention to your "core"—abdomen and lower back—as this is generally the weakest region for cyclists.
- Cool down gradually (10–20 minutes or more of low-intensity aerobic exercise). Ideally, this would be on a stationary bike, emphasizing a sustained, high-cadence effort.

Third, effective resistance-training programs, regardless of sport, are "periodized." This means that the resistance-training program follows a predictable progression or pattern of overload, designed to elicit a specific training result (much as do the various interval routines you perform on the bike).

As resistance increases, the repetitions decrease. A simple method to determine the relative difficulty of a phase is to multiply repetitions by sets by weight. Generally, the transition phase should have the lowest difficulty, followed by the high-volume phase (based on increasing the number of sets, as opposed to weight), and then by the strength phase (based on increasing the amount of weight lifted).

Power workouts are usually reserved for on-bike resistance training. This allows the cyclist to take the strength gains out of the gym and develop power on the primary tool of the sport—the bicycle. CTS coaches prescribe a number of different workouts for this purpose, including PowerStarts (PS), StompIntervals (S), MuscleTension intervals (MT), and One-Legged pedaling (OL). These workouts can be incorporated throughout your off-season resistance-training program as an adjunct to what you are accomplishing in the gym. They are also emphasized during a 2–4 week power phase at the end of resistance training.

The fourth guideline for effective resistance-training programs is that they should include multiple-set efforts (usually between three and six) that are unique to each phase of resistance training, as opposed to programs that prescribe single sets to exhaustion, which are not periodized. A common mistake is to not allow enough time for recovery between sets. A minimum of one minute is recommended, and as the resistance and/or number of sets increases, the recovery time should be increased to two minutes. If you don't allow enough recovery time, you will fatigue prematurely, and the quality of the overall workout may be diminished.

Finally, the fifth guideline that any program should be built around is the current physical development of the individual athlete.

By paying attention to these guidelines, any cyclist should be able to demonstrate noticeable strength and power gains on the bike as a result of resistance training in the off-season.

CHAPTER 19

THE "GREAT INDOORS"

How to Get the Best Out of a Magnetic-Load Trainer

CHRIS CARMICHAEL

Last fall, as Matt Kelly watched the Wisconsin days grow shorter and colder, he was forced to deal with reality:* The season was winding down, and winter was rapidly approaching. Many of you are faced with this same situation, and for some, the off-season could last as long as six months. Eventually, you will be forced to do at least some of your training rides indoors. Although these may not be the most picturesque or exciting rides, they are a valuable part of your training program.

Rather than focus on the approaching change of season, Kelly took advantage of this opportunity to maximize his training time. During the winter, he completed all of his training in the basement of his parents' home. The indoor workouts he performed allowed him to concentrate on the demands of competition and ultimately led to a gold medal in the world junior cyclo-cross championship.

In fact, it is a good idea to do indoor workouts year-round. You can use outdoor rides to build and maintain an aerobic base, and use indoor workouts to develop lactate tolerance and buffering capacity and to increase anaerobic power. At least once a week, you should be reaching for a favorite compact disc and a portable fan.

* This article first appeared in slightly different form in *VeloNews* 28, no. 20 (1999)

Indoor workouts offer several advantages over those performed outdoors. First, you will have a high level of repeatability. By using a magnetic-load trainer and a downloadable heart-rate monitor, you will have the ability to reproduce workouts. In other words, each time a particular workout is executed, you will be doing it exactly the same way. These training tools also allow you to monitor the quality of your exercise closely and compare one session to another. Second, riding indoors permits you to have strict control over your environment. Under these conditions, you will not have to deal with the wind, terrain changes, darkness, unfavorable temperatures, aggressive dogs, or traffic. This setting lets you direct your attention to the task at hand, which is performing high-intensity efforts.

Warm-Up

Each training session should be divided into three parts: the warm-up, the workout, and the cooldown. It is imperative that each aspect is included in order to ensure a high-quality workout. The warm-up should take 20 to 30 minutes. During that time you should include two to three short but intense efforts. Do the same warm-up each time—this will ensure the repeatability of your workout. The warm-up is also a good time to check the placement of your fan and to make sure you have adequate ventilation.

Maintaining a steady flow of air will keep you from overheating and prevent cardiac drift, which is an increase in heart rate in response to hot environments. Cardiac drift can adversely affect the relationship of heart rate to power output, which can limit your ability to generate maximal power. This potential problem makes an electric fan an essential part of your indoor training regime.

Intervals

Once a proper warm-up is complete, it is time to begin the interval portion of the session. There are several options from which you can choose; the following is just one example. If an athlete needs to increase anaerobic power, lactate tolerance, and repeatability during short, intense efforts, I like to prescribe CTS DescendingIntervals (DI). DIs consist of short, maximal efforts with recovery periods of equal length. One set entails the following:

- 120 seconds maximal effort followed by 120 seconds recovery
- 105 seconds maximal effort followed by 105 seconds recovery
- 90 seconds maximal effort followed by 90 seconds recovery
- 75 seconds maximal effort followed by 75 seconds recovery
- 60 seconds maximal effort followed by 60 seconds recovery
- 45 seconds maximal effort followed by 45 seconds recovery
- 30 seconds maximal effort followed by 30 seconds recovery

These are short, maximal efforts, so you must have an explosive start. Choose a moderate gear for these intervals, one that allows you to maintain a relatively high cadence — 110 rpm or higher. Begin out of the saddle, and then sit down to increase your speed as the interval progresses. Remember to maintain the proper cadence. If needed, shift to a lighter gear to maintain the appropriate cadence and intensity for the interval.

The elevated cadence will cause your heart rate to be extremely high, and will train your muscles to produce large amounts of power over repeatable efforts. With this in mind, do not worry about your heart rate during this workout. It is more important to focus on putting out a maximal effort. The recovery time is short, and therefore you will never fully recover before the next interval begins. This helps you develop the ability to tolerate lactate accumulation in your muscles.

Workouts like this are of great importance to Kelly. He performs two to three sets of DIs with 10 minutes of easy spinning between sets. These short, intense efforts help him prepare for the demands of the cyclo-cross season. Keep in mind that these are difficult workouts, so I recommend doing only one or two sets the first couple of times.

Cooldown

The final piece of the workout is the cooldown. Resist the urge to hop off your bike and head to the refrigerator for a cold beverage. Instead, prepare a bottle of your favorite recovery drink before you begin the workout, and drink it while you do a light spin for 20 to 30 minutes. This active recovery will help return pooled blood to your heart and bring oxygen-rich blood to your working muscles. The combination of these two elements will aid recovery and restoration.

If you are using a heart-rate monitor that can be downloaded, this can be a good time to examine the data from the workout. Your average heart rate during each interval and the heart's recovery rate are of particular importance. Use these values to compare this session with previous and future training sessions, thus giving you repeatability and the capacity to monitor changes in your fitness level. As your fitness improves, you will be able to see quicker heart-recovery rates along with greater ease in maintaining high heart rates during each interval. So, step inside and enjoy the "great indoors"!

CHAPTER 20

BOOSTING EARLY-SEASON FITNESS WITH TEMPO WORKOUTS

CHRIS CARMICHAEL

You started the off season with good intentions and a solid winter training plan.* You spent plenty of time logging base miles. You vowed to avoid jumping into an intense training program without building enough base miles in your legs. So far, everything is going well for you; slowly and steadily you have increased your training mileage and resisted the urge to show off during the January and February club rides.

At this point of the season, you have a couple of training races under your belt, or you may be preparing for the first racing series. Your main goals for the season may be 10 to 14 weeks away, but you know that it is time to increase training intensity. But what's next? Intervals, sprints, climbing repeats? And how do you maintain endurance and aerobic conditioning while getting ready for this month's races? These are good questions and never completely easy to answer whether you have the first spring racing series next week or at the Milan–San Remo race in March.

* This article first appeared in slightly different form in *VeloNews* 28, no. 4 (1999).

Tempo

After plenty of base miles, it is time to boost your current fitness level with tempo training. Tempo workouts involve training at higher heart-rate intensities than you did while logging base mileage. This intensity may be known as an athlete's aerobic threshold, a term considered outdated by some sport scientists. Dr. Ed Burke, author of *Serious Cycling* (Human Kinetics Publishers) describes tempo intensity as follows:

> *The initial phase of exercise is predominantly aerobic with a heavy reliance on slow-twitch muscle fibers and glucose and free fatty acids as the primary metabolic fuels. The aerobic threshold leads to the aerobic-anaerobic transition phase, which involves the recruitment of oxidative fast-twitch fibers and the appearance of lactate in the blood above resting levels and greater reliance on blood glucose and muscle glycogen. The aerobic-anaerobic threshold transition phase ends at the anaerobic threshold where lactate production equals its removal capacity. The anaerobic phase follows. This phase involves the recruitment of glycolytic fast-twitch fibers with a rapid rise in lactic acid formation. Lactate production exceeds its removal with a rapid increase in blood lactate.*

The Benefits

Tempo workouts that are strategically placed in your training program have many advantages:

- Greater comfort while the peloton is cruising on rolling terrain
- Better fuel utilization during long races
- Increased workload capacity for more intense forms of training
- Increased power output at moderate cycling intensities
- Increased muscle glycogen storage capacity

- Improved free fatty acid oxidation, sparing muscle glycogen
- Increased mitochondria, structures within the muscle cells that produce energy
- Improved aerobic capacity and efficiency

Too Much of a Good Thing?

The key to tempo workouts is understanding that you need extensive training at the tempo intensity in order to get positive returns. This huge volume of training at subthreshold intensity will provide the best adaptations. Also, be aware that this form of training can easily lead to overtraining. Many athletes experience quick returns from tempo workouts. Elite athletes like Lance Armstrong experience an increase in subthreshold power output following a two-day tempo-training block. Clearly, these athletes are the exception and not the norm. Elite athletes adapt quickly, but I have observed similar results from non-elite-level athletes, who reap the benefits of tempo training but sometimes fail to recognize the toll this training can take.

Too much tempo training with too little recovery can lead to fatigue and overtraining symptoms. Since the training intensity feels more like a "slow drain" of energy and not the white-hot intensity of training at lactate threshold or greater, tempo workouts tend to sneak up on you. If you don't allow for proper recovery, you soon will feel the dreaded effects of overtraining. Once you have completed a training phase of tempo workouts, change your workouts to emphasize higher speed, pedal cadence, and fluidness. Tempo workouts will make you feel strong enough to mash the pedals all day like a diesel engine, but expect to be short on speed, acceleration, and peak power.

Getting Started

Before adding tempo workouts to your training program, make sure you have plenty of base mileage in your legs. I normally advise elite athletes like Armstrong to have at least six weeks of base mileage before building tempo workouts into their training programs. Master's national champions Laura Lindgren and Allan Crawford, who train one to two hours a day, will normally have a greater number of weeks (8–10 weeks) spent building up base mileage. This ensures deeper general fitness before heading into more intense training.

Calculating Intensity

Among the methods for determining your tempo intensity, some are more accurate, and some are more convenient. Generally, I use physiological testing such as a VO_2 max or lactate threshold test to help establish the heart rate and power output to use as levels for the correct training intensity of tempo workouts. Normally for elite athletes, this is between 70 to 78 percent of VO_2 max, and between 65 to 70 percent of VO_2 max for non-elite-level athletes. During a recent VO_2 max and lactate threshold test for George Hincapie, we established tempo training intensity at 162–164 heart rate and 330 watts power output. This intensity also corresponded well to a perceived effort for Hincapie as "somewhat to moderately hard" but below-threshold intensity. If you decide to go this route, it's critical that you see a qualified sports medicine professional who is also well versed in testing cyclists and interpreting test results.

Physiological testing is often out of reach for most athletes. Calculation of tempo intensity is commonly done using the Karvonen method or using a percentage of maximum heart rate. An easy and quick approach is to use a riding pace that you can sustain for 20 to 30 minutes without riding at your lactate threshold. If, after five minutes, you have the feeling of burning in your legs, heavy breathing, and nonstable heart rate, you are riding too hard. Tempo intensity is below lactate threshold heart rate and well below your time-trial heart rate, but is hard enough that you are uncomfortable, as if there is a slow drain of your energy. You will experience the tempo workouts getting more difficult the longer you spend at tempo intensity. Many athletes feel fine during the first 15 minutes, but it slowly takes greater effort to maintain the desired intensity. The last 15 to 30 minutes can be downright tough. I suggest using riding pace and perceived exertion with heart rate to get the best results in determining and monitoring your tempo intensity.

Structuring Your Program

Tempo training yields the greatest results with large training volume at tempo intensity. I have found from the athletes I coach that tempo workouts structured into two-day training blocks, followed by two days of recovery riding, allow a sufficient training load with ample time for recovery. If you have only a limited amount of time for training, a three-day training block will give you an additional workout. The length of the tempo workouts for the first training block is usually 30 to 40 percent of the total volume of the training session. As you begin adapting to your tempo workouts, you can continue to enjoy power gains if you consistently add more volume. If the athletes show no signs of difficulty in handling the tempo workouts, I increase the length of them by 5 to 10 percent for the third and fourth training block and add the same increase for the fifth and sixth training block.

Recovery

The recovery days between tempo workouts should include easy riding on flat or rolling terrain, maintaining a normal pedal cadence and low heart rate. The key is to ride enough to provide active recovery but not so hard as to apply a training stress. Many times I include a series of three to five short sprints of 8–10 seconds on the second recovery day. I find it useful in maintaining leg speed and coordination during a heavy tempo-training phase. As long as the sprints are short and you give yourself plenty of recovery time between sprints, you won't tax yourself much. After six solid training blocks of tempo workouts, training shifts to other types of workouts in order to boost your overall performance.

Technical Considerations

Since tempo training generally begins early in the cycling season, before you head into race-specific training, pedal speed can be lower. Try a 70- to 75-rpm range while staying at the correct tempo intensity. This helps increase pedal resistance and strengthen the leg muscles. I also recommend staying in the saddle when you hit hills during your tempo workouts. This adds more pedal resistance and readies connective tissues and other supporting muscle groups before training heads into more explosive workouts.

Not only will long climbs challenge you physically during tempo workouts, but you should also expect that you will need to increase your heart rate by 3–8 bpm. Many athletes experience higher heart rates on long climbs while maintaining the same perceived effort as riding on flat terrain.

CHART 1: **GEORGE HINCAPIE**

	Monday	Tuesday	Wednesday	Thursday	Friday	Saturday	Sunday
WEEK 1	4 hours w/90 mins tempo @ 162–164 HR	5 hours w/120 mins tempo @ 162–164 HR	Recovery day	Recovery day	4 hours w/5–6 stomp intervals	5 hours w/120 mins tempo @ 162–164 HR	Recovery day
WEEK 2	Recovery ride	4 hours w/100 mins tempo @ 162–164 HR	5 hours w/135 mins tempo @ 162–164 HR	Recovery day	Recovery day	4 hours w/5–6 stomp intervals	5 hours w/135 mins tempo @ 162–164 HR
WEEK 3	Recovery day	Recovery ride	4 hours w/100 mins tempo @ 162–164 HR	5 hours w/145 mins tempo @ 162–164 HR	Recovery day	Recovery ride	4 hours w/5–6 stomp intervals
WEEK 4	5 hours w/145 mins tempo @ 162–164 HR	Begin recovery 5 days phase	Recovery ride	Recovery ride	Recovery ride	Recovery ride	4 hours w/MT intervals

CHART 2: **LAURA LINDGREN • ALLAN CRAWFORD**

	Monday	Tuesday	Wednesday	Thursday	Friday	Saturday	Sunday
WEEK 1	Day off	1 hr w/20 mins tempo Allan HR: 154–156 Laura HR: 172–174	1 hr w/25 mins tempo Allan HR: 154–156 Laura HR: 172–174	1 hr w/30 mins tempo Allan HR: 154–156 Laura HR: 172–174	Recovery ride	2–2 1/2 hrs club ride with race-like efforts	4 hr endurance ride w/HR ceiling: Allan: 158 Laura: 175
WEEK 2	Day off	1 hr w/30 mins tempo Allan HR: 154–156 Laura HR: 172–174	1 hr w/35 mins tempo Allan HR: 154–156 Laura HR: 172–174	1 hr w/40 mins tempo Allan HR: 154–156 Laura HR: 172–174	Recovery ride	2–2 1/2 hrs club ride with race-like efforts.	4 hr endurance ride w/HR ceiling: Allan: 158 Laura: 175
WEEK 3	Recovery day—rest up for the upcoming Los Angeles to San Francisco ride	Recovery ride—rest up for the upcoming ride	Recovery ride—rest up for the upcoming ride	Endurance ride, LA to SF	Endurance ride, LA to SF	Endurance ride, LA to SF	Endurance ride, LA to SF

Included here are examples of tempo workouts for a few of the athletes I coach (see Charts 1 and 2). Notice the steady progression of tempo workouts, the individual training intensity, and the critical recovery days after the training blocks. Note that these are the individualized training programs of each athlete, and thus other forms of training appear in the charts; these are based on each individual's characteristics, goals, and objectives for the season. Do not randomly follow any of these training programs; they have not been designed for you.

Feedback

An important element of any athlete-coach relationship is communication. Here is the text from a typical email from Karen Kurreck after a training ride:

I finished another tempo ride. It was about 3 1/2 hours with 1 hour 45 minutes tempo. Heart rate was kind of low and took a long time to come up, I think because the last two days have been kind of hard. I rode more on feel than heart rate. My speed on the same terrain (at the same heart rates) was quite a bit faster than it has been. I was pretty much able to hold the tempo intensity for the whole 105 minutes except going downhill. I finished with a long climb (36 minutes), so it was a bit easier to keep heart rate up in the end.

- First 16 minutes rolling (average heart rate 154).
- 24-minute climb (average heart rate 160).
- 22-minute gradual descent where I could pedal most of the way. I had to stop in the middle because of a construction light. Before the stop (10–15 minutes), my average heart rate was 161. After the stop, there was more downhill and it took a while to get heart rate back up (average heart rate 149).
- 36-minute climb (heart rate 160).

I rolled home after the last climb and felt pretty good about the day's efforts.

CHAPTER 21

SEEING IS BELIEVING

Vision Correction Options for Cyclists

DR. RICHARD S. KATTOUF II

You're on a descent, hitting speeds over 40 mph, with a 90-degree turn at the bottom.* Suddenly, your glasses fog up. . . .

If you're a cyclist who wears glasses or contact lenses, you're well aware of the special problems you face in a sport where clear vision is critical. Cyclists are exposed to a great deal of wind, which often carries debris. If this debris lodges underneath a contact lens, it can cause severe discomfort and affect your vision and depth perception—not something you want during training or racing. Eyeglasses offer an alternative to contacts, but they bring their own host of problems: Eyeglasses get dirty, broken, lost, scratched, or fogged—usually at the worst possible moment.

Fortunately, whether you are nearsighted, farsighted, or astigmatic, there are now a number of ways to attain clear vision without wearing contact lenses or glasses. In our ever-progressing high-tech world, refractive surgery and accelerated orthokeratology (Ortho-K) lead the way in vision correction.

Laser vision correction (Lasik) is a state-of-the-art surgical procedure that corrects nearsightedness, farsightedness, and astigmatism. Ortho-K is a

* This article first appeared in slightly different form in *VeloNews* 30, no. 3 (2001).

nonsurgical procedure that corrects nearsightedness and astigmatism. Both procedures eliminate the need for either eyeglasses or daily-wear contact lenses.

Lasik works by reshaping the curvature of the cornea with a laser, thereby improving the patient's distance vision. The procedure is pain-free and has a low percentage of minor side effects, such as dry eye and halos around lights. Laser vision correction is not a lengthy procedure. Once you are on the operating table, a skilled surgeon can complete the surgery in approximately three to five minutes per eye. The recovery time from Lasik surgery is also minimal. There's a good chance that you can be back on your bike the next day.

For those cyclists who are apprehensive about having surgery on their eyes, Ortho-K is an excellent option. This procedure corrects nearsightedness and astigmatism through the use of a specially designed gas-permeable contact lens that is worn only at night while you sleep. By wearing this reverse-geometry molding contact lens, your cornea is flattened and your vision gradually improves. The lens is removed upon awakening and you enjoy clear vision throughout the day.

An accelerated orthokeratology contact lens is larger than an ordinary gas-permeable contact lens but smaller than a soft contact lens. Patients often experience some lid sensitivity during their first few nights of wear. This lid sensitivity will dissipate each night. The process is similar to that of wearing braces for the teeth. When a patient's braces are removed, a retainer is worn in order to keep the teeth in place. Your Ortho-K contact lens can be compared to the braces and retainer combined. The lens serves to mold your cornea and help it retain its shape as time goes on. Depending on one's prescription, an orthokeratology contact lens is worn anywhere from three nights to seven nights per week.

Those of you wearing bifocals may wonder if either of these procedures will correct your near-vision. This depends on your prescription. Some near-sighted patients can opt to have monovision performed with either Lasik or Ortho-K. Monovision involves correcting your dominant eye for improved distance vision while modifying your nondominant eye for improved near-vision. With both eyes open, you are able to adapt to this type of vision. However, this option presents possible problems: Some patients are unable to adapt to monovision, due to compromised distance-vision, compromised near-vision, or both. Other patients may experience decreased depth perception. Because depth perception is critical in cycling, monovision is not the correction of choice for cyclists.

Of the numerous patients I have examined after they've undergone either Lasik or Ortho-K, the results and satisfaction have been extremely high. Patients experience incredible joy once they achieve clear vision without their contacts or glasses. Being able to train and race without wearing visual correction can be a life-changing experience.

I know this first-hand. After 21 years of wearing contact lenses—since I was seven years old—I chose to have laser surgery. Ortho-K was not an option for me because I was too nearsighted. I chose Lasik because as a multisport athlete, I liked the idea of training and racing without contact lenses.

I couldn't be more satisfied. My vision is extremely clear, both day and night. Dr. Edmund Burke, the renowned sports physiologist and author, recently had Lasik as well. He told me he achieved 20-20 vision five days after his surgery. In regard to the side effects, Burke reported some cornea dryness and fluctuating vision, which is improving each day. Fluctuating vision is common during recovery from Lasik surgery and is characterized by relatively rapid changes in vision, from focused to blurry to out-of-focus. This symptom, which is caused primarily by excessive corneal dryness, gradually lessens and disappears altogether after a few days.

Meanwhile, there also have been great advances in conventional vision-correction procedures. Contact lenses now correct nearsightedness, farsightedness, and astigmatism. If you wear bifocals and are unable to see your cycling computer, bifocal contact lenses and monovision correction could be a solution. The latest development in contact lens technology is uniquely tinted lenses that provide sun and glare protection.

If contact lenses, Lasik, or Ortho-K does not fit your lifestyle, prescription sports eyewear is your best option. Clear lenses and a multitude of tinted lenses are available for just about any light condition. A good all-weather lens is one that is tinted persimmon. This lens provides adequate glare protection on sunny days, yet also enhances vision on overcast days. Mountain bikers perform well with this lens, because their rides include wooded and shaded trails combined with more open, sunny areas. Some companies offer removable prescription inserts for their sport frames, which are good alternatives for contact-lens wearers. But no matter which lenses you buy, be sure they offer ultraviolet protection. Ultraviolet light from the sun can cause premature damage to the eye.

Cycling is a high-speed, potentially dangerous sport. Clear vision minimizes the risks involved. Whichever vision correction you choose, consult a qualified optometrist and ophthalmologist and gather as much information as possible to help you make a decision.

CHAPTER 22

ARE YOU READY?
TEST YOURSELF

CHRIS CARMICHAEL

fter an early spring during which he was besieged by illness and crashes, Lance Armstrong was finally able to gain a solid block of racing and training.* The Amstel Gold Race in the Netherlands was to be Lance's first goal of the season and was just two weeks away. We wanted to test his fitness level to evaluate his training progress and to help determine how competitive he would be. I had plenty of subjective data based on his daily workouts and racing data to aid in the comparison. What was lacking were strong objective measurements based on the individual physical components that would contribute to his overall performance.

It was impractical for Lance to head into a lab to conduct a VO_2 test or a lactate threshold profile. We needed a simple field test that was repeatable and noninvasive and that would accurately reproduce and measure the same critical demands he would face during competition. An important critical demand faced by endurance cyclists is the amount of maximal work that can be sustained for at least 30 minutes. This usually places them somewhere above their lactate threshold or at an intensity that I call "individual race threshold."

* This article first appeared in slightly different form in *VeloNews* 28, no. 16 (1999).

The field test that I use with Lance is a steep, 12-kilometer climb close to his home in Nice, France. It is best to have the field-testing location within 10 to 15 kilometers of an athlete's home. This helps ensure repeatability and makes it practical for athletes to perform the test often. Repeatability is of great importance to field testing. It begins two days out from the field test, with a reduction in the training load so that the legs are fresh and ready to perform. I like to prescribe the exact volume and intensity for the workouts two days before every test.

The advent of power meters like the SRM has enabled athletes to use the simplest form of field testing an uphill time trial to evaluate the critical components of success. From these components, I can draw powerful conclusions in regard to race threshold power, watts per kilogram, and heart-rate intensities.

Two weeks before the Amstel Gold Race, Lance posted a very quick time on the test hill, producing higher sustainable power at similar heart rates compared with his previous test. I then divided his average power production by his body weight and was able to establish his watts per kilometer at race threshold pace. This is a critical value for all cyclists. From this information, we knew that Lance was responding well to his training and racing. If he were to continue to lose a selected amount of weight, we knew we could still expect improvements in his watts-per-kilogram value. We also knew he was beginning to reach a high level of fitness and could expect a strong performance at Amstel Gold. The rest is history: Lance rode very well to finish second.

Field testing before any major event is important. It is best to test five to seven days before a targeted event and during the beginning of a new training cycle. However, field testing is a double-edged sword. It provides real numbers that are good indicators of your fitness level, but the numbers can indicate good or bad news.

It is possible to conduct a race threshold test indoors or outdoors. As I have described, the outdoor field test can be either a long climb or 30-minute time trial. Using a magnetic-load trainer such as the Blackburn RX-8, along with a power meter, you can reproduce a similar field test indoors. The difference between the two is that the indoor field test will aim to estimate your lactate threshold heart rate and power at threshold. The indoor field test will not give you what I call your individual race threshold or maximal sustainable power. Both tests are valuable, but expect different power output numbers from each.

Getting Ready

- Ease up and reduce training intensity and volume two days before the field test. Always try to reproduce the same workouts each time before you conduct the field test.

- Always conduct the same warm-up routine before every field test. I advise at least 30 minutes of warming up with at least one 3- to 5-minute effort just above lactate threshold.

Field Test—Outdoors

- You always want to reproduce the same test as you did before. Try to conduct the field test when the wind is relatively calm and the temperature is warm, and make sure the test is done at a time of day that will be convenient for you in the months to come.

- Do not eat for at least three hours before your test. During the last 45 minutes before your test, drink a sports drink to boost energy levels and to aid in hydration. As always, eat the same as you did for the last test.

- Don't worry too much about the start. Just roll to your starting point at a slow pace and accelerate quickly, but not too quickly. Give yourself at least four minutes to reach your maximal sustainable pace. Don't forget to start your power meter's marker at the start of the field test.

- Just as in a normal time trial, select a gear that allows you to maintain a cadence between 95 and 100 rpm (crank revolutions per minute) on flat terrain, or 85–90 rpm if climbing. Avoid the impulse to mash a big gear at slow rpm; the greater resistance will build more leg-burning lactic acid. The secret is to use the gearing that is most efficient for your personal riding style. Most athletes will respond better to using a slightly lighter gear than what they are accustomed to. Watch your power, cadence, and heart rate as you use different gearing to help establish optimum pedal cadence.

- Settle into your pace and try to avoid any quick accelerations, as this can drive you above your maximal sustainable pace and soon your legs will begin to load with lactic acid. Settle into a steady rhythm of breathing. From here it's going to hurt, but remember it is a sustainable effort for at least 30 minutes. This will produce a different sort of pain than sprinting does.

- As you head to the finish area, don't forget to stop the power meter's first marker and to time your ride to the nearest second. Record the weather conditions, gearing used, and your perceived effort for the test.

- To finish your field test, cool down with an easy spin at a low heart rate for at least 30 minutes. This is also the time to begin the recovery process by drinking a sports drink to help speed your recovery.

This field test will give you important information on your fitness. Taking your average heart rate over the course of the entire test will establish your race threshold intensity. This heart-rate intensity will normally be above your lactate threshold. I usually roll back the heart-rate intensity by five to eight beats per minute and use these heart-rate values for prescribing heart-rate intensities when aiming to increase an athlete's lactate threshold. I have found that there is little value to increasing an athlete's lactate threshold by training at race threshold intensities.

Another important data point established with this test is the ability to monitor increases in average power output at a given heart rate. Look for the same or similar heart-rate values but an increase in the power you are able to produce. This means you have made increases in power output along with greater efficiency of lactate clearance at lower heart-rate intensities. Both of these are valuable and very trainable characteristics for endurance cyclists. After each field test, record the following:

- Time of the field test
- Average power output for the field test
- Average heart rate during the field test
- Maximal power and heart rate during the field test
- Weather conditions for the field test
- Perceived effort for the field test
- Your body weight the morning of the field test, just after waking

Over time, you and your coach will be able to use this information to establish conclusions about the effectiveness of your training program and your fitness level and to make adjustments as necessary.

George Hincapie went into the 2001 Paris-Roubaix with excellent form and proved he was the strongest man in the race, but in the end he was outnumbered and had to succumb to the three Domo Farm-Frites riders.

CHAPTER 23

ALL ROADS LEAD TO ROUBAIX

CHRIS CARMICHAEL AND
GEORGE HINCAPIE

There have been few fluke winners of Paris-Roubaix.* It's a race that allows only the day's strongest rider to emerge victorious. In a way, that makes George Hincapie's preparation straightforward: Develop the strength and power to sustain a massive effort for six hours. The training goals may be uncomplicated; the race is anything but.

The Challenges

The Hell of the North is an apt nickname for this race: It's over 260 kilometers long, the race conditions can be horrible, and there are those famous 26 sections of centuries-old cobblestones, or *pavé*. The challenges the pavé sections present can be more of a problem than the stones themselves.

When the race hits the first pavé after about 100 kilometers, there are huge advantages to being among the first 20 riders onto it. For one thing, you have a clear line of sight, allowing you to pick a good line through the cobblestones. For another, there is considerably less risk of getting caught in or behind one of the inevitable crashes.

* This article first appeared in slightly different form in *VeloNews*, 30, no. 5 (2001).

Since everyone knows how important it is to be at the front, the fight for position starts early and gets heated. Even though the field thins out as the race progresses, the battle for position remains intense throughout the race. George compares it to fighting to win a field sprint in a super-fast criterium, 26 times in one day.

There is no "sitting in" during Paris-Roubaix. It is rare to stay on anyone's wheel for any extended period of time, let alone hide in the peloton. Instead, riders face frequent accelerations and maximal efforts as they leapfrog each other on the narrow cowpaths of northern France. This creates two challenges. First, George has to be able to put forth efforts at or near his maximum repeatedly, for hours, with little recovery between efforts. Second, he has to recognize when and how to make those efforts.

George's mental suitcase of past scenarios, acquired over seven Paris-Roubaix appearances, gives him the ability to "ride by wire." Experience has taught him how to handle the cobbles, the weather, his bike, and the miles. As a result, George can maintain focus on the race as a whole and make good decisions as to when to use his strength and power.

Targeting the Challenges

In the weeks before the race, George's training includes workouts that target its particular demands. DescendingIntervals (DI) develop his capacity for repeated maximal efforts. They are hard on the body and must be carefully balanced with rest. A typical DI workout for George may include several sets of six intervals, starting at 3 minutes and getting shorter by 30 seconds each interval. The recovery time between intervals begins at 3 minutes and decreases at the same rate as the interval time.

Another essential workout is PowerIntervals (PI), which address the maximal power demands of the race. PowerIntervals PIs are relatively long maximal efforts (4–5 minutes) with short recovery periods (3–4 minutes) and are only effective at building a rider's peak power when there are strong support systems to build upon. Accordingly, in the late winter, George was riding long Tempo (T) and SteadyState Intervals (SS) to build his aerobic engine and develop his capacity for producing power at lactate threshold.

As with DI, PIs are very stressful and need to be balanced with more recovery time between workouts. I always give George at least 48 hours between workouts of this intensity. George's typical PI workouts include four sets of three 4-minute intervals, with 3 minutes of recovery spinning between intervals and 10 minutes of recovery spinning between sets.

Descending Intervals and Power Intervals are useful additions to anyone's training program but only after a foundation has been laid. Adding such intense intervals too early in a training program, without energy systems strong enough to support them, often leads to below-average returns and above-average fatigue.

As a general guideline, I would recommend that a Category 3 or Masters competitor begin with two sets of DI, starting with a 90-second first interval and reducing each of the following five intervals by 15 seconds. Recovery time between intervals is the same as the length of the previous interval (90 seconds maximal effort, 90 seconds recovery, 75 seconds maximal effort, 75 seconds recovery, etc.). Recovery between sets is 10 minutes of easy spinning.

I would recommend that the same group of athletes start with two sets of three PowerIntervals. Start with 3-minute intervals separated by 5 minutes of recovery spinning. Allow 10 minutes of easy spinning for recovery between sets. I've used the Category 3 and Masters groups as an example because they are a good reference point for other groups on either side of the fitness and experience scale. Over a period of three to four weeks, riders should progress by first adding time to the intervals; second, reducing recovery time between intervals; and third, adding more sets of intervals.

Race Day

One compartment of George's mental suitcase holds his habits and routines. He knows how to eat, dress, warm up, and focus, no matter what is going on around him. When the race starts, George will be ready. The following is George's own take on Paris-Roubaix:

Paris-Roubaix is intense from the gun. Staying out of trouble in the early going is important, so I try to ride near the front and near my teammates. As we approach the first pavé, there is a lot of bumping and shoving. The race starts going faster and faster as riders accelerate toward the front to avoid getting caught in the bottleneck at the start of the pavé.

I keep my cadence high at the beginning of the race and through the first sections of pavé, trying to spare my muscles for the later parts of the day. The carbon fiber Treks help a great deal; they are much more forgiving than the bikes Chris rode in his day. By the time you get to the last few sections, you have to do whatever is necessary to keep your speed up, so it is important to have something left in your legs.

The pavé sections are central to what Paris-Roubaix is all about, but they constitute only 50 kilometers of racing. You have to be aware of where you are and who you are with when you exit the pavé because the breakaways often occur on the smooth roads.

The Arenberg Forest is an especially critical part of the course. It comes about two-thirds of the way through the race, with about 100 kilometers and about 10 pavé sections to go. The crowds are huge and the course can be really rough. You have to focus and hold the throttle wide open.

Gaps open quickly late in the race, and it is sometimes hard to tell who has the energy left to cross them. The easiest gap to close is the one that never opens, so staying alert and reacting quickly become more important as everyone tires. Riders start testing each other for weakness a long way out from Roubaix; for example, Johan Museeuw attacked 50 kilometers from the velodrome in 2000.

I would love to come into the velodrome alone in front, but even if I am part of a small group entering the final five kilometers, I feel confident in my ability to win. A strong team and a great director are critical in Paris-Roubaix, and this year I think we have one of the strongest teams and the best director, Johan Bruyneel, for this race. I'm ready.

CHAPTER 24

ROAD TRIP
Staying Fit While Traveling
CHRIS CARMICHAEL

Y ou've been following your coach's instructions all season—training right, eating well, getting plenty of sleep—and you're excited about an upcoming ride or race.* Then the boss walks in, tosses a dossier on your desk, and informs you that you're the project lead on a nine-day, five-city tour. Your hard-won fitness flashes before your eyes, replaced by visions of cramped economy-class plane seats, three-martini corporate lunches, and late-night number-crunching sessions.

Hey, it's life, and a lot of life is about work. Just because travel is hard on you and your form, it needn't be the death sentence you think.

Stay Calm

First, think things through. Where are you going? Can you take your bike? What times of day (or night) will you be free to work out? Next, ask whatever travel service you're using to create a traveler profile for you. Request things such as bulkhead seats (more leg room), hotels with gym facilities, and special meals on flights.

* This article first appeared in slightly different form in *VeloNews* 29, no. 7 (2000).

You might consider purchasing a foldable travel bike, or a kit that can convert nearly any steel road frame into one that is foldable. Neither option is cheap, but both will allow you to check your bike as standard baggage, eliminating oversize fees. If you can't bring your bike, check the hotel workout facilities; measure your saddle height and cockpit length so that you can adjust the stationary to your normal position. And for any trip, pack your shorts, shoes, and pedals—and don't forget a pedal wrench.

Remember to stay hydrated while training. It's particularly easy to develop a chronic case of dehydration when spending both working and training hours indoors. Try a hydration system that is easy to use, clean, and a constant reminder to drink.

The Workouts

You're going to be crunched for time, so concentrate on quality over quantity. VO$_2$ max workouts provide an excellent "maintenance" program—you won't get a lot faster, but you'll preserve your current fitness. The two workouts I recommend for my athletes are SteadyState Intervals (SS) and PowerIntervals (PI). Three of these workouts over the course of a week-long road trip will help you maintain most of your fitness and be bike-ready when the trip's over. All workouts should be preceded by a 10- to 20-minute warm-up, with several intervals of hard riding that are less intense than the workouts.

SteadyState Intervals (SS)

Goal: Increase lactate threshold (LT) by training at the edge of your aerobic-anaerobic threshold.

How to do it: This workout can be performed on hills, flat terrain, or an indoor bike. Intensity is at your individual LT, or 80–85 percent of your maximum heart rate, slightly below your time-trial effort. It's critical to maintain this intensity for the length of the SS Interval, as interruptions limit the benefits.

Pedal Cadence: 70–80 rpm on hills, 85–95 rpm on flats or indoors. Maintaining intensity is more important than maintaining cadence.

Do: Efforts of 10–20 minutes, with 8–12 minutes of moderate-cadence, low-gear spinning as rest between reps. Two to three reps per workout. (Total time: 1 hour to 1:50.)

PowerIntervals (PI)

Goal: Increase power output during short intense efforts.

How to do it: Perform on an indoor trainer or stationary bike for controlled environment, or find a flat stretch of road. Intensity will be about 88 percent of your maximal heart rate, or slightly above your time-trial effort. Take one minute to build up to the desired training zone, then maintain that intensity throughout the interval.

Pedal Cadence: 110 rpm or higher. Maintaining pedal cadence is crucial in this workout. If you have to, shift to a lighter gear to maintain cadence, but do not let the intensity of the interval drop. With a high cadence, your heart rate will remain extremely high, and you will train the body's ability to deliver oxygen to the muscles. This workout was key to George Hincapie's success in last year's spring classics. Training at higher cadences and intensities allowed him to attack on hills late in races, when everyone else was gasping for breath.

Do: Four to eight three-minute intervals per workout, with four minutes of easy spinning as rest between intervals. (Total time: 38 minutes to 1:16.)

Stuff to Remember

When you're on the road and working, life generally feels more stressful. So listen to your body. If you're feeling tired, don't push it—just get on the bike and do an easy spin at a low heart rate. And do less volume of intensity than you would at home: Three of these workouts a week is plenty. You'll do much more harm by going hard and getting sick than by pulling back a bit until your trip is over.

It's also important that your meals be as healthful as possible. Don't be afraid to ask for specific food. Without turning into the proverbial ugly American, you can pleasantly order from off the menu. If all the listed dishes are high in fat and protein, ask for a bowl of pasta with olive oil instead. Most restaurants can easily create such simple dishes, and asking for them does not make you a pain for the serving staff or your dinner partners. They'll probably be interested in your reasons for ordering specials and be respectful of your dedication to cycling.

Like anything else bike-related, travel requires adapting to different situations. Professional racers endure numerous setbacks and distractions over the course of a season. You can too. If you listen to your body and train wisely, travel doesn't have to mean the end of your world—or of your fitness.

CHAPTER 25

THE ART OF FIELD SPRINTING

Or How to Win Races and Influence People

GEORGE HINCAPIE

First, you should know that field sprinting is no exact science.* A thousand things must go perfectly right for you to win. Above all, field sprinting is about two things: preparation and awareness. You must go into a race knowing everything you can possibly learn about the race, your opponents, and yourself. During the race, you have to be as aware as possible of any factors that can influence or change your desired outcome. Here's my plan.

Preparation

First things first: You must know the race. All of my races have final kilometers laid out in the handbook or race bible. Since only top-level races have bibles, it's best in other cases that you preride at least the final parts of the course. I memorize the corners in the last kilometers, especially with one kilometer to go. If you can see the finish, that's great, but it's not always possible, so you have to know where the turns are and what the finishing straight is like. Is it uphill? Wide? Is there a corner 75 meters from the line? All these factors will affect your positioning in the pack entering the sprint.

---

* This article first appeared in slightly different form in *VeloNews* 29, no. 9 (2000).

Next, you want to know your competition. Who are the strong riders? Who's a good sprinter? Which are the good strong teams? This can be harder to determine at lower levels of amateur racing, where team tactics don't play in as much, but often there's at least one team whose goal is to get to the finish in a group. If you know there's a team with a good sprinter, then rely on its members to help control the race. If you don't know that, you're taking a risk relying on help from anyone.

Finally, know your team. If its planned tactic for the day is to set you up for a sprint, have confidence in your teammates to chase breaks down and put you in a good position for the final sprint. The corollary to that is the harder they work for you, the more you want to win for all the work they did. Use that as motivation.

How I Train for Sprinting

To build my power, Chris Carmichael prescribes weight workouts in the winter—squats, leg presses, and cross training—and I also do CTS's top-end power workouts, such as Stomps and PowerStarts, after my foundation period. It's important to note that you should have a good aerobic base before trying these workouts—they're very high-intensity, and you run the risk of injury if you attempt them "off the couch." The recovery times are long because you need to clear the lactate out of your muscles. If lactate remains in the muscles, your peak-power output is reduced. This is not good for improving top-end speed. The key is peak-power output: The muscle adapts to peak power, just as it does when you lift weights, so the heavier the load, the stronger the muscle becomes.

High-Speed Sprints

- *Goal:* To develop top-end power and speed.

- *Terrain:* Slight downhill.

- *Cadence:* 110-plus rpm.

- *The workout:* Roll at 25–30 mph in a big gear; jump out of the saddle and accelerate. When you top out the gear, return to the saddle and focus on maintaining high cadence and good form for the entire sprint.

- *Do:* 1–3 (beginner riders) or 4–6 (advanced) efforts of 8–12 seconds each, with 8–12 minutes for recovery between sprints.

Flat Sprints

- *Goal:* To develop acceleration, body's use of ATP (instant-energy) system.

- *Terrain:* Flat road.

- *Cadence:* High (using a relatively light gear at approximately 20 mph).

- *The workout:* Spin along at about 15–22 mph and jump out of the saddle, accelerating the entire time; then, after a few seconds, return to the saddle and focus on maintaining a high cadence and smooth form over the sprint.

- *Do:* 2–3 (beginner) or 4–6 (advanced) sprints of 8–10 seconds in length. Recover 5–10 minutes between sprints.

Stomps

- *Goal:* To increase power during in-the-saddle efforts (the final part of a field sprint).

- *Terrain:* Flat road, preferably with tailwind.

- *Cadence:* Not applicable. Use a large gear (about 53x15 to 53x12).

- *The workout:* Start at about 15–20 mph and, remaining in the saddle, begin stomping on the pedals as hard as possible. Concentrate on smooth, circular pedal strokes.

- *Do:* 2–3 (beginner) or 4–8 (advanced) Stomps of 15–20 seconds each, with 8–10 minutes recovery between each Stomp.

PowerStarts

- *Goal:* To increase muscular power and transfer to the bike.
- *Terrain:* Flat section of road.
- *Cadence:* Not applicable. Use a large gear.
- *The workout:* Begin at a near standstill. Jump hard on the pedals, out of the saddle, for 8–12 seconds. Ride as hard as you can.
- *Do:* 2–3 (beginner) or 4–8 (advanced), with 5 minutes recovery between sprints.

During the Race

Keep a cool head. You did your homework on the race and your competition. There are a couple of things to consider during the course of the race:

1. Stay toward the front. Big races get really crazy, and you want to stay out of the craziness so that you don't waste energy. Aim to be in the top 15 percent of the field, and always keep a teammate or two near you to help out if something happens. Use lighter gears, spin more, don't push the gear, eat and drink enough, and do all the normal, typical things you'd do to conserve your energy.

2. Stay vigilant. What's going on ahead of you, behind you, around you? The road might get narrow and stretch out the pack, or there's a wind change, and you can feel the surge from riders behind you. Surges occur when there's a speed decrease at the front of the field because of a headwind or some other factor, and guys start to come around you. Don't let that happen; if you let one or two guys in front, you could be 20 riders back in seconds. Keep your position in a pack. (Note: At the 1999 Tour de France, Alex Zülle was in the latter half of the field on stage two and was caught behind a crash at a narrow causeway crossing. He lost about six minutes on the stage and was never in

contention for the overall, although his final deficit to winner Lance Armstrong was only 1:30 more than the time he lost on that one stage. Stay at the front.)

3. Breakaways—what do you do? Again, this comes back to homework you do before the race. You will have to take risks and know that you won't be able to go with a break and still conserve your energy. I usually won't go in a break any farther than 10 kilometers out. If some riders go up the road, it helps to know what their strengths are—not necessarily how they feel that day, but in general, so you know if you can beat them. You often need this information late in a race if you're in a smaller group of riders. If you're confident that you're a better sprinter than another rider, conserve your energy; you may be able to lead out and not have guys come around. Conversely, if he's stronger, make him work more. You're always playing a game with each field; every situation is different, and you have to improvise.

The Final Kilometers

It's crunch time, and the pack is riding faster and fighting for position. Rely on your guys to keep you in position, and have one guy up there as a designated lead-out. Stay on his wheel and let him steer you through traffic.

Lots of guys like to get on some big sprinter's wheel, but it's always too hectic behind riders like Mario Cipollini or Erik Zabel, so I stay with a teammate rather than fight for that wheel. Often, some guy will try a last-ditch flyer to stay away. As with earlier breaks, it's a judgment call. If the pack speed is really high, then stay in. The guy will probably get reeled back in, but if you think he's going to make it stick, then you have to make your decision fast if you want to cross that gap.

5 Kilometers Out

There's no etiquette or respect for having a wheel—even in the pros, and even less in amateur racing. Pack speed has gotten really fast, and there's a lot of bumping, which at those speeds can make your ride touch-and-go. Make sure to establish your position near the front and not let the bumping bother you.

Now you'll need to start using your energy to stay at the front; the situation will be much like the from-behind speed surges I mentioned earlier. Know the course, and start paying close attention to what's happening around you. Do not let anyone take the wheel you're on.

1 Kilometer Out

Once you flash under that banner, think quickly about what's left—you did your homework, so you know the last few kilometers. Speed has gotten really high, and you want to be at the front but sheltered. If you come out in the wind going this fast, you'll go straight backward, so stay on that wheel.

Check conditions. Is the wind coming from the left? If so, pass your lead-out man to the right to use him for shelter. If you have a headwind, can you stay on the wheel longer? Is there a better side to come around on?

Last 500 Meters

Full go. Up to this point, you need to know what's going on around you. But now you're operating on feel, and you can't do much about what's happening around you anyway. I try to get in a zone in the sprint where I don't let anything bother me. I know my team is doing 100 percent for me, so I give 100 percent back. In your mind, just remember that this last 500-meter stretch is your job. No matter how hectic things get, don't get distracted. If a thousand things have gone perfectly right, you'll win.

PART FOUR

RECOVERY

CTS member Will Frischkorn takes a corner in the USPRO Criterium Championships in Downers Grove, Illinois. Will has been working with Chris Carmichael since he was 17 years old.

Introduction to Recovery

JIM RUTBERG and
WILL FRISCHKORN

Will Frischkorn has been working with Chris Carmichael since 1999. Will progressed from a very talented junior to a national-caliber senior in a short time. His teammates on the Mercury Cycling Team taught him a lot, as did Chris and several other mentors. Some things, however, must be learned through experience. Will had to learn to read his body and interpret his needs as an athlete.

One of the biggest challenges for young athletes is realizing how much rest and recovery they need. Their natural tendency is to push themselves extremely hard in an attempt to match the training of their older, more experienced teammates. There is also a desire to prove to everyone that they can handle huge training and racing loads. Will learned about the importance of recovery the way that most young athletes learn — through exhaustion. Will described his experience this way:

I was racing the Grand Prix de Beauce in Canada in June 2000. My legs felt good out on our recovery spins, but the instant we started racing, I knew that the form I had just a week before was long gone. When I was riding at a high tempo, up to about my lactate threshold and even just a bit over, I was OK, but the second I really started to dig, my legs filled instantly and turned to lead. On the stage with a mountaintop finish, I dug a bit too deep early in the climb. By the top, I might as well have been walking.

Scott Moninger was flying during that race, and we started riding tempo to support him. I thought, "Perfect, I can do this—no problem." Then the pressure was on. It was the last day of the race, and the other teams decided that the win wasn't going to be Scott's so easily. A potentially winning break-away went up the road, and we had to pick up the pace in the main peleton. Ouch. I mashed the biggest gear I had trying to use every available muscle. My normal heart rate at threshold is 185, but I was stuck in the high 160s pedaling as hard as I could. My heart rate would not come up; I felt I was pedaling through wet cement.

As we approached the finishing circuits, the breakaway was still too far up the road, and we had to give it everything we had. On the flats, I could maintain enough speed and power, but the second we hit even the smallest rise, I was straight out the back. Fortunately, the field was big and stretched out into a long line of riders, so I could tuck into the draft, get some rest, and make my way back to the front. For the next 30 kilometers, my race consisted of the following: Ride hard, hit a hill, go backward, struggle forward, pull for the team, hit a hill, go backward, and so on.

We finally made it to the first climb on the finishing circuits, and I watched as the pack pulled away at three times my speed. I knew that by reaching the finish line, I would grab the young rider's jersey as the highest-placed rider under 23 years old. The other riders in that competition were still somewhere behind me on the road. I focused on keeping the cranks spinning. My legs hurt, everything hurt, but I finished. Then I tried to get off my bike. My legs could barely hold my weight. I slumped into a chair and, after getting some food and water, tried to figure out why that day had been so hard.

All spring I had been doing lots of miles on the bike and a lot of Tempo workouts. I always felt good after a few of those workouts. I figured I needed to go home, take it easy for a day, and then put in some serious Tempo workouts. Two weeks before the race in Canada, I had the best form of my life. Some hard training would bring that form back; that's how it works.

I called Chris Carmichael to see what he thought. After I described the way my legs felt, he told me, "Five days off the bike. That's what you need. Then do some good foundation work, and you'll be fine." That wasn't exactly what I was expecting, but that's what a coach is for—a second, often smarter perspective. This time it was about letting the body recover a bit, something I had been neglecting. Five days off never felt so good, then after some solid miles and quality base work at altitude, the legs were back. What do you know—the coach was right.

CHAPTER 26

BACK OFF, BUDDY

How to Avoid and Treat Overuse Injuries

ERIK MOEN, PT, CSCS

ost cyclists have experienced a few aches and pains along the way.* Most of the time, these just come with the territory, and some rest is all you need. Sometimes, though, the aches and pains can grow into something more serious: overuse injuries.

Overuse injuries are prolonged rubs, grinds, and tears of soft tissues that cause pain and limit riding. As the name implies, they occur over time and are caused by irregular or excessive forces applied to a soft tissue such as cartilage or tendons.

Overuse injuries may also occur as a result of an improperly rested acute injury. Common overuse injuries include tendonitis, cartilage degeneration, pain syndromes, peripheral nerve irritation, and muscle tears. A more extensive list is included in the last section of this chapter.

These injuries often creep up slowly, and their effects on performance are progressive. While the pain may seem innocent at first, dysfunction related to an overuse injury often worsens dramatically, leaving the athlete in a state of depression.

* This article first appeared in slightly different form in *VeloNews* 30, no. 9 (2001).

Bicycling-related pain syndromes do not have to occur, but a "ride through the pain" attitude will only make things worse. By observing a few precautions, you should be able to enjoy the sport relatively pain-free for years to come.

When Do Injuries Occur?

If you think about the mechanics involved in cycling, it's almost surprising that there aren't more overuse injuries in the sport. The bicycle is supposedly a symmetrical object, which your somewhat symmetrical and, I hope, flexible body is supposed to fit onto. Then, you pedal with force for hours upon hours. At 80–90 revolutions per minute, that's about 15,000 pedal turns over the course of a three-hour ride. It's a recipe for overuse.

What are the main culprits in overuse injuries, and how can you prevent them? Common mechanisms of injury include training errors, musculoskeletal anomalies, and bike-fit irregularities. Training errors are a large part of overuse injuries. These errors can fall into two categories: physiological errors, and pedagogy or technique errors.

Physiological errors usually involve excessive increases in volume (miles or hours of training) and intensity (heart rate) without proper recovery, a guaranteed route to injury. Hard work is a necessary part of our sport, but care must be taken when advancing training variables. The general rule with regard to intensity and volume is to decrease one while increasing the other.

The act of pedaling a bicycle is part of bicycling pedagogy. Pedaling techniques are important, as pedaling is a high-force and highly repetitive motion. Common pedaling errors include quad bias pedaling (aka mashing the pedals or pedaling squares) and prolonged low cadence (less than 80 rpm). Ideal cadence for endurance riding is 80–100rpm.

Musculoskeletal anomalies are imperfections or challenges of our muscles, tendons, bones, and joints. Anomalies limit our ability to ride a symmetrical bicycle with force over time. They fall into three groups: flexibility, weakness, and asymmetries.

Flexibility is one of the most overlooked training methods in the sport of bicycling. Good flexibility of the legs and spine allow for pedaling with few motion compensations. Motion compensations frequently become evident in rotations of the leg as the foot passes through the dead-bottom-center of the pedal stroke. This is why cleats with float are necessary for some. Cyclists are most commonly inflexible in the hamstrings.

Weakness or imbalance of muscle groups can also be a stimulus for injury. The most common weaknesses are of the hamstrings relative to the quadriceps, the gluteus medius (lateral hip muscle), and the lumbar extensors. A well-balanced hamstring group helps stabilize the knee joint under forceful extension of the leg (pedaling), and then helps clear the leg across the back of the pedal stroke.

The role of the gluteus medius is to help guide femoral direction and stability in pedaling. It helps prevent the knee from drifting to the inside during the pedal stroke, otherwise known as a valgus moment at the knee. The lumbar extensors are the base of support in cycling. They serve to anchor the torsion of a somewhat upright posture, and they are responsible for providing a base of support for the production of leg force and the transfer of that force to the pedals. Weakness of trunk musculature allows for greater irregular joint-loading and extremity/spine motion during pedaling.

Musculoskeletal asymmetries provide challenges to a person attempting to fit on a symmetrical bicycle. Common body asymmetries arise from such things as flexibility differences, strength imbalance, and structural differences. Body asymmetries often cause one-sided injuries. Leg-length differences are a common form of body asymmetries and can arise from differences in tibial length or femoral length or from pelvic dysfunction.

The most common bike-fit errors include improper saddle height, improper handlebar reach, and misalignments of pedal and shoe. A good bike fit should consider individual musculoskeletal challenges and features. Once your bike is fit to you properly, write down the specific measurements so that you can dial in your position after disassembling your bike for traveling, making repairs, or installing new components.

Treatment

The treatment of an overuse injury depends on the individual case. The sooner you identify an overuse injury and the sooner you start to fix it, the sooner you will be back to pain-free cycling. Imagine being a detective. How did you develop the injury in the first place? This information will help you tailor your rehabilitation plan to the specific needs of the injury.

Recovery and treatment require modified rest. Effective treatment will include aspects of flexibility, anti-inflammation, strength, biomechanics, and nutrition. The retraining of pedaling skills should be included. Possible intervals should include one-legged pedaling and fast pedaling. Controlling variables such as gearing, heart rate, cadence, and terrain can help, too. Consider making it a habit to have a complete physical at the completion of a competitive season. This physical should include physiological markers, cycling biomechanics, and musculoskeletal examination. Attention to observed deficits in your seasonal training plan will allow for greater performance gains over the following season.

The key to injury-free performance is the athlete's ability to discern and report irregular pain and dysfunction. The body is adaptable to a certain point. Attempts to push the body past the point of adaptation will lead to injury and/or pain-induced performance reduction. Be safe, be smart, train right.

Common Overuse Injuries

Anterior knee pain, illiotibial band tendonitis, spinal pain (neck and lower back), hamstring tendonitis, and extremity (hand and foot) numbness/pain are among the most common overuse injuries. Here are some of the reasons they occur:

- Anterior knee pain: low saddle, low cadence, quad bias pedaling, mis-aligned cleat, and muscle imbalance (strong quads, weak hamstrings)
- Illiotibial band tendonitis: high saddle, leg-length difference, and mis-aligned cleat
- Neck pain: long/low handlebars, short-reach handlebars, and down-ward tilt of saddle
- Low back pain: inflexible hamstrings, low cadence, quad bias pedaling, poor back strength, and long/low handlebars
- Hamstring tendonitis: inflexible hamstrings, high saddle, misaligned cleat, and poor hamstring strength
- Hand numbness/pain: short-reach handlebars, poorly placed brake levers, and downward tilt of saddle
- Foot numbness/pain: quad bias pedaling, low cadence, faulty foot mechanics, and poor cleat placement

Conrad Stoltz rides to victory at the 2001 Boulder Peak Triathlon.

CHAPTER 27

FLUID DYNAMICS

Without Sodium, Water Can Overwhelm Your Body

J I M   L E H M A N

Water bottles pop up like flowers when summer turns up the heat, as sweaty athletes try to keep their parched bodies refreshed.* But where proper hydration is concerned, more is not always better . . . and believe it or not, it is possible to drink too much water.

The most abundant substance in our bodies, water is involved in chemical reactions, absorbs and releases heat, and serves as a lubricant. Losing just 2 percent of your body's water can hamper your athletic performance.

A corresponding loss of sodium while you sweat through a strenuous workout or race on a blistering summer day can be a good deal more dangerous than simple fluid loss—it can serve as an invitation to gastric distress, seizures, and even death.

While you exercise in the heat, your body tries to maintain a constant core temperature by increasing the rate at which you sweat. This is an excellent heat-regulating mechanism, but it also strips vital sodium from your body. If you are consuming water only during your workout or race, you run the risk of diluting the sodium concentration in your blood, a condition called hyponatremia, or water intoxication.

* This article first appeared in slightly different form in *VeloNews* 30, no. 11 (2001).

This condition typically occurs in ultradistance events, but it has also been seen in events lasting just three to four hours. Other individuals who may be at risk are athletes who compete in multiple events in a single day, such as the masters racer who does the 35+, 45+, and the Pro1 and 2 criteriums on a Sunday afternoon.

If this sounds like you, it is essential that you understand the importance of sodium and the role it plays in your bodily functions. Remember, if you can't finish, you can't win.

Sodium Spreads Fluids Around

Sodium is an electrolyte that is necessary for water balance, cellular metabolism, and muscular contractions. It draws water through permeable membranes and distributes fluid throughout the body.

When your body loses sodium through sweat, it also loses some of its ability to move water across these membranes. This will eventually lead to dehydration—even if you are drinking plenty of water.

Without sodium, that water will not be distributed properly throughout your body, and you will feel bloated, nauseated, and unable to perform to the best of your ability. Other symptoms of hyponatremia can include headaches, cramps, extreme fatigue, disorientation, and slurred speech. If these symptoms are allowed to progress, they can lead to seizures, coma, brain damage, and even death.

Plan a Rehydration Strategy

To avoid such a situation, you must develop a strategy for water and salt consumption. Your goal should be to replace the same amount of fluid you lost, or will lose, during exercise.

You can estimate your fluid needs by weighing yourself before and after a strenuous workout, in conditions similar to those you will experience during your event. Weigh yourself in the morning after you have gone to the bathroom, and then again after your workout. It is important to be consistent with your measurements. For every pound lost, consume one pint of fluid. As the saying goes, "A pint's a pound the world around."

If you maintained or gained weight during your workout, you probably consumed too much water and may be experiencing reduced blood sodium. You should eat sodium-rich foods as part of your recovery process to re-establish an electrolyte balance. Do this gradually over the course of the next 10–12 hours. During this time, your body will increase urine production to rid itself of the excess fluids.

Before and During the Race

If you are preparing for a race, you need to increase your water consumption for several days beforehand to minimize the risk of dehydration. You should also increase your sodium ingestion by 10–25 grams per day, which will help prevent your greater fluid intake from diluting sodium levels in your blood.

During the event, you should take about a gram of sodium each hour. Most sports drinks have only 100–200mg of sodium per serving, so you will need to supplement these with sodium-rich foods. Be cautious with salt tablets; it's easy to get too much sodium with them. Make sure to do your experimentation during training rather than on race day.

Skip the Pain Relievers

Using aspirin, ibuprofen, or acetaminophen can contribute to hyponatremia.

Many endurance athletes use these drugs before and during competitions in an effort to prevent or minimize pain. But they can interfere with your kidneys, which help regulate your body's water content, so it's better to wait until after your event to seek a little pain relief.

Managing your water and sodium intake so that you are replacing only what you have lost will not only help you turn in a better performance come race day but also will keep you out of the medical tent afterward. Then you can spend your postrace hours relaxing at the local cantina, enjoying a jumbo order of chips and salsa — an excellent source of sodium.

MID-TERM BREAK

How to Stay Focused During the Season

D E D E   D E M E T - B A R R Y

T he end of the Hewlett-Packard International Women's Challenge marked the midpoint of my 2000 race season.* After racing 45 days, sleeping 101 nights in unfamiliar beds, hopping planes, driving to race starts, and punishing my body in rain, cold, heat, and humidity, I was exhausted.

Cyclists are always on the move during race season. We become accustomed to the high-paced rhythm of a demanding lifestyle, and most of us thrive on the adventure. Inevitably we feel a little burned out at some point, and it's easy to lose focus. I say "inevitably" because there is no separation between mind and body. We race as complete people, and we fatigue as complete people. The key to maintaining form throughout a long season is knowing when to take a break.

Burnout: Symptoms and Signs

As athletes, we are competitive at heart. We have a fire inside of us, we are hungry to race, and we are eager to push our limits and win. Races are often won and lost on mental strength. At the elite level, everyone is an excellent

---

* This article first appeared in slightly different form in *VeloNews* 29, no. 14 (2000).

athlete, and it is often the mental edge that separates the winners from the rest of the peloton.

Overtraining and burnout are most frequently recognized by the loss of competitive hunger and motivation. Knowing when to rest is the key to maintaining form, as is making sure you are always fueling the competitive fire by keeping it fun. You must know yourself well and be able to recognize the signs of fatigue.

What's the difference between being tired from a race and being tired of racing? It is normal to feel tired after each race. Racing a bicycle requires a huge effort, and you are usually riding at your limits, which means digging deep into your reserves. Your body has a built-in gas tank: The more you dip into your reserves, the more you deplete the tank. You tax your body on a regular basis throughout the season.

With deeper fatigue, you begin to lose focus. Your results begin to suffer, and you start dreaming of the off-season, chocolate ice cream, and lounging with your friends in a nonsporting environment. That's a sign your mid-term break has arrived. Rest, sleep, and a proper diet will help get you through the rough times—and back to winning ways.

What to Do

Take a few days off to rediscover the reasons you started cycling in the first place. Leave your bike in the basement and go for walks in the park, see new sights, enjoy old friends. Soon enough, you'll be itching to start pedaling like a mad person again.

Upon arriving home in Boulder, Colorado, after the Hewlett-Packard race, I felt beat. I rode into my reserves during the two-week race, and the mental and physical stress took a lot out of me. My coach, Chris Carmichael, told me to take it easy, rest, recover, and recharge the batteries. So I chilled at home. The first day I napped on and off, ate three solid meals, and read with my legs in the air. I felt drained. My body had shut down and was in full recovery mode.

Over the next few days, I pedaled around town on my city bike with my husband. We stopped for naps by the creek and tossed the Frisbee in the park. Each time I stepped on the bike served as a massage for my legs, nothing more—a simple spin to keep the blood flowing in my body and make sure my legs didn't seize up. While I was resting up, I also got a few massages and ate well: no cakes or sugary foods but lots of organic salad, grains, and meats. I try to vary my diet and eat different proteins, vegetables, and starches at each meal so that I can get a full spectrum of nutrients and vitamins.

What About Your Fitness?

The hardest part of taking time off is the worry that you will lose fitness. Cyclists, and most athletes for that matter, are addicts. When we are not riding, we are worrying about the next race and our form and fitness. To feel happy, we must deplete ourselves, test ourselves, and burn up our surplus of endorphins. Have no fear. As long as you eat and rest properly, no form will be lost during three or four days of complete rest. Keep this in mind and relax as much as possible.

Without rest and recovery in your program, you will encounter a big wall at some point in the year, a wall that is incredibly hard to scale. Injuries, as well as mental and physical burnout, are some of the consequences of overtraining and insufficient rest. Your body and mind are sacred, and you must preserve your well-being if you want to be a champion.

Balance is key to finding long-term happiness as an athlete. The cycling season is simply too long and too challenging for anyone to endure at full bore. Take time to enjoy your family, friends, and hobbies. Your cycling benefits when you keep your other interests alive. Most of all, you'll continue to love your bike and won't reach the point where you want to chuck it off a bridge.

CHAPTER 29

RECOVERING FOR BETTER TRAINING

Sometimes to Get Faster, You Have to Go Slower

JIM LEHMAN

You finish your third interval workout of the week and lean your $3,000 bike against the wall.* As you turn on the tv, you remove your high-tech performance clothing and $175 shoes. Sure, you're surrounded by equipment and clothing of value, but you're forgetting a valuable part of your training program: muscle recovery.

While you are channel surfing, your muscles are patiently waiting for your attention. They have just endured a punishing regime, one designed to make them stronger and you faster. For that to happen, they need your close attention. Now is the time to re-establish fluid and electrolyte levels, replace depleted energy stores, decrease oxidative and muscle stress, and rebuild muscle protein. Recovery is a critical aspect of training, and one that many athletes fail to address properly.

Training is based on stimulus and response. To go faster, you must, at times, go slower. In fact, you become stronger as a result of the recovery process rather than during the intense training sessions. The training session provides the muscle stimulus, or stress, and the recovery phase allows the muscles to respond or adapt

* This article first appeared in slightly different form in *VeloNews* 29, no. 6 (2000).

to the training. It's this combination of workouts and recovery that make up the training process.

Many cyclists believe they are going to lose fitness if they take a day off, so they continue to train. But neglecting recovery ultimately means losing fitness as your body becomes unable to handle the training load. When this begins to happen, you will become fatigued and unmotivated and headed toward a state of overtraining. Some signs to watch for include weight loss, restlessness, loss of appetite, muscle soreness, inability to maintain your focus, elevated resting heart rate, and disruption in your sleep patterns.

A training diary can help you and your coach recognize these signs. You should record your morning heart rate and weight to establish a baseline. Sleep is also critical to your recovery, so you should track the number of hours you sleep each night. If you find yourself sleeping less than eight to 8–10 hours, you may be hampering your recovery. To bolster the process, indulge in an afternoon nap if you can. This will revitalize and re-energize you, both physically and mentally.

Recovery can be divided into three phases: before and during exercise, immediately after exercise, and long term.

Recovery Before and During Exercise

The first phase begins with an adequate warm-up and a good stretching routine to minimize muscle trauma and facilitate recovery. A proper warm-up will raise body and muscle temperature; increase blood flow and availability of oxygen to working muscles; increase heart and breathing rate; and mobilize free-fatty acids as a fuel source, thus sparing glycogen.

During the training session, try to drink 20 to 40 ounces of fluid each hour. Although this will not match the fluid lost during exercise, it will help limit dehydration. If the ride lasts longer than 60 minutes, you should also consume a carbohydrate energy drink. There are a few things to look for in a sports drink. First, you need to like its taste. If you don't, you probably aren't going to drink it. Second, it should be at room temperature so that it doesn't slow down gastric emptying. Finally, the beverage should be a 6–8 percent carbohydrate solution. If you buy a powdered drink, be careful how you mix it, since the label recommendations are often above this range.

Each ride should conclude with 10 to 20 minutes of light spinning. During this time, your body begins to return to its resting levels: Heart and breathing rates drop, body temperature decreases, metabolism levels off, ATP levels are restored, and lactic acid is removed. Low-intensity pedaling also helps maintain steady blood flow to the muscles, which enhances recovery.

Recovery Immediately After Exercise

While you are exercising, your body uses carbohydrate, fat, and protein as fuel, with carbohydrate being the primary source. After exercise, these stores are depleted and must be replaced to advance your training. The two hours immediately after your training session are critical, particularly the first 30 minutes. This is often referred to as the "glycogen window."

During this time, your muscle cells are hypersensitive to insulin, the hormone that transports blood glucose to the muscles. At the same time, insulin stimulates the conversion of glucose to glycogen, so that it can be stored in the muscles and liver. It's important to take advantage of this period and rapidly replace the depleted glycogen stores. Research has shown that you can enhance the insulin response by combining carbohydrate and protein. In his book *Optimal Muscle Recovery* (Avery Publishing Group, 1999), Ed Burke states that the ratio should be 4:1—4 grams of carbohydrate to 1 gram of protein. This allows protein to stimulate the insulin response without hindering fluid absorption or gastric emptying.

You should ingest 1 gram of carbohydrate for each pound of body weight. Try to consume foods that are high on the glycemic index—bananas, bagels, raisins, and sports drinks. These foods are readily digested and have a rapid impact on blood glucose levels, which stimulate insulin to replenish glycogen stores.

This is also the time to replenish the fluids and electrolytes lost during exercise. The body needs water for temperature regulation, maintenance of plasma volume levels, and proper cardiovascular function. Losing as little as 5 percent of your plasma volume can lead to diminished performance. Regardless of how much you drink during your workout, you are not able to replace fluids at the same rate as they are lost, which leads to involuntary dehydration. After your ride, you need to drink 20-24 ounces of fluid per pound of body weight lost. Drinking water will help, but water alone is not sufficient. Plain water dilutes the electrolyte concentrations in the blood, which suppresses your desire to drink before you have re-established your pre-exercise fluid and electrolyte levels. Therefore, your post-exercise drink should contain electrolytes, specifically sodium, potassium, and magnesium.

Training and racing provide the stress needed for your fitness level to improve but can also cause muscle trauma and damage. As you exercise, you accumulate free radicals. These highly unstable molecules are largely responsible for the damage called oxidative stress that occurs within the muscle. Vitamins C and E are effective antioxidants. They help limit free-radical buildup and the subsequent damage and inflammation that can occur. With proper recovery, your muscles will repair themselves and become stronger.

Although your body tends to use carbohydrate as its primary fuel source, when its glycogen stores are depleted, it must tap into protein stores. This results in muscle damage and causes you to experience muscle soreness. So for your training to progress, you must rebuild these damaged muscle proteins. The branched-chain amino acids (bcaa) isoleucine, leucine, and valine are vital components of muscle proteins and are needed to promote muscle protein formation and repair damaged tissues. This rebuilding process begins immediately following exercise. Once again, insulin plays a major role: It stimulates muscle protein synthesis and promotes glycogen storage. Since the typical American diet contains adequate amounts of protein, you shouldn't have to supplement your diet, unless you are under heavy racing or training stress.

Long-Term Recovery

The final phase of recovery occurs 2 to 20 hours after your training session. During this time, you should focus on ingesting complex carbohydrates, which will provide a slow and steady supply of glucose. Choose foods that are low to medium on the glycemic index, such as apples, oatmeal, figs, and dates. Try to consume 3–5 grams of carbohydrate per pound of body weight. Within two to four hours after training, you should eat a high-carbohydrate meal to help stabilize your glycogen stores and prepare you for the next day's workout.

This long-term phase is when the muscles rebuild themselves and, ultimately, when you become faster. You should also continue to pay attention to your hydration levels, so maintain your water intake.

If you monitor your recovery and continue to work hard, you will achieve and perhaps surpass your performance goals. And hey, if you are willing to spend money on high-end equipment, don't neglect the most important piece of equipment you own: your body. Spend some of that cash on a massage and recover, recover, recover.

CHAPTER 30

STRATEGIC RECOVERY

During the Heart of the Racing Season, Recovery Is Key to Continued Success

CHRIS CARMICHAEL

Summer brings warm weather and hot racing.* At this point in the season, you can expect to be racing two to three times per week, and you must remind yourself that it is the racing that you're working toward, not the training.

Racing is your best training. You gain tactical improvements and learn when and how to use these tactics. Racing intensities develop speed, speed endurance, and high power output. However, you must be careful to maintain a proper ratio of recovery and training between your races.

As athletes head into the summer, they often are riding very well. Their racing schedule begins to look something like this: Saturday and Sunday races, with the inclusion of a mid-week training race. There is no problem with a schedule like this, but what happens between these races can either make or break a season. Often cyclists continue a heavy training load between races, thinking that they must continue to ride the same number of training miles they were logging earlier in the season. Wrong.

* This article first appeared in slightly different form in *VeloNews* 28, no. 8 (1999).

The days between races should be filled with riding, but it must be at a reduced training load, and special attention must be paid to nutrition. Races place a much greater stress on your body than does training. The total volume of time spent at or above lactate threshold while racing is high, and the greater this time, the more time is needed for recovery. For example, Lance Armstrong spent more than two hours at or above his lactate threshold during the 1996 Flèche-Wallonne. This is a huge volume of intensity, and he would be tackling Liège-Bastogne-Liège four days later.

Lance never duplicates such an effort in training, and he needed extra rest in order to recover from the taxing event. The same concept applies to everyone; you will always reach beyond yourself while racing. Between races, rides should be shorter and less intense. The rate at which an athlete recovers from races and hard workouts depends greatly on factors such as fitness level, physical aptitude, nutrition, weather, and the stresses of the most recent race. Some athletes respond better to taking a full day off the bike, and others prefer active recovery riding. The table shown here offers some guidelines for planning and establishing the quantity of recovery time to schedule between races and hard workouts. These times should be treated as only a starting point. How quickly you recover from racing or intense training depends on many factors and will be individual.

Volume of intensity	Suggested time needed for recovery
0–6 hours at aerobic endurance intensity	8 hours
30–60 minutes at tempo intensity	8–10 hours
75–120 minutes at tempo intensity	24–36 hours
15–45 minutes at lactate threshold	24 hours
60–90 minutes at lactate threshold	24–36 hours
10–30 minutes above lactate threshold	24–36 hours
45 minutes or more above lactate threshold	36–48 hours

Recovery Begins Immediately

The moment you cross the finish line is the best time to jump-start the recovery process. It is crucial that the proper nutrients in the right proportions be ingested before, during, and after a race. It is in the interval between races that your adaptations for increased muscle strength and endurance occur. Consumption of carbohydrates, specific proteins, and other supplements during and after exercise can bridge the gap between potentially excessive racing, training and exceptional performance, and recovery. Your ability to perform repeatedly at peak levels during the racing season is limited by how quickly muscles recover and repair themselves after each race.

After reading Dr. Ed Burke's book *Optimal Muscle Recovery*, I found the new science-based model for optimizing muscle recovery—the R4 System—to be interesting and helpful because it offers a simple approach. By understanding the science behind the following four principles of the R4 System, you can make enormous strides in improving recovery and performance:

- Restore electrolytes and water
- Replenish glycogen stores rapidly
- Reduce muscle and oxidative stress
- Rebuild muscle protein

Restore Electrolytes and Water

Fluid and electrolyte replenishment is crucial to maintaining cardiac output and regulating body temperature during exercise. Elevations in your body temperature can sharply impair your performance. Studies have shown that fluid replacement must occur both during and after exercise. Electrolytes usually found in sports hydration drinks can accelerate rehydration by speeding intestinal reabsorption of fluids and improving fluid retention. The key electrolytes are sodium, potassium, and magnesium. Often your thirst mechanism is insufficient to motivate you to restore fluid and electrolyte balance.

Replenish Glycogen Stores Rapidly

Immediately after a race, replenish glycogen stores. Early studies focused primarily on replenishment of glycogen stores by consumption of a carbohydrate supplement both during and after exercise. The regulator of glycogen replenishment is the hormone insulin, which increases the transport of glucose from the blood into the muscle and stimulates the enzyme responsible for the conversion of glucose into glycogen. Insulin is so important in recovery from exercise that it should really be called the "master recovery hormone."

Recent studies have shown that combining a carbohydrate supplement with protein and the amino acid arginine will stimulate both insulin levels and glycogen replenishment. The ideal carbohydrate-to-protein ratio is extremely important to obtain this synergy. The optimal ratio should be 4:1—4 grams of carbohydrate for 1 gram of protein. By further stimulating insulin, you can restore muscle glycogen more quickly.

Reduce Muscle and Oxidative Stress

The muscle cell undergoes considerable trauma during races. This trauma leads to soreness and the need to rebuild protein. It is only recently that the causes of oxidative and muscle stress have been defined. During exercise there is a buildup of free radicals. This is called oxidative stress. Free radicals are largely responsible for damage to the muscle cell membrane.

Antioxidants such as vitamins C and E have been shown to reduce free-radical buildup during exercise and protect against muscle damage. It is common in the middle of the racing season, when physical stress is at its highest, for athletes to compromise their immune system, making them more susceptible to colds and infection. The natural herb ciwujia and the amino acid glutamine have both been shown to stimulate and boost the immune system.

Rebuild Muscle Protein

Repair of damaged muscle proteins begins immediately after exercise. Insulin stimulates muscle repair by increasing amino acid transport into the muscle. During a heavy racing period, extra protein to help offset tissue damage can be helpful.

In his book, Burke notes that branched-chain amino acids make up one-third of muscle protein and are involved in the body's response to stress and the building of muscle. Sufficient amounts of branched-chain amino acids are found in any quality whey protein supplement.

A critical aspect to recovery is to replace the carbohydrate and protein within the first 30 minutes following your races. Your body is several times more capable of absorbing and replenishing these fuels immediately following the race than at any other time.

What to Do on Days Between Races

Full recovery between races may take on a different protocol for each athlete, but the concept remains the same — ride enough to stimulate active recovery but not so much that you introduce a training load upon yourself. The few days between races are not the time to seek increased training volume.

Simple rides of 30–120 minutes at a low heart rate and a comfortable pedal speed will aid recovery. For example, after winning the 1996 Flèche-Wallonne race with three days until the Liège-Bastogne-Liège World Cup, Lance Armstrong did the following recovery riding:

Thursday 75 minutes easy spin at 75–80 rpm, 112 average heart rate

Friday 60 minutes easy spin at 75–80 rpm, 115 average heart rate

Saturday 2 hours with two short efforts of 5 minutes at 178–183 heart rate, 2 minutes recovery between efforts, 118 average heart rate

The riding Lance did was at a low heart rate and power output so that he did not induce training stress but instead helped speed the recovery process. This entailed increasing blood flow, accelerating the inflow of nutrients, reducing muscle soreness, and relaxing his mental state by spending quiet time on the bike.

The day before the Liège-Bastogne-Liège race, Armstrong did two short efforts above lactate threshold. This helped "open him up." Such workouts activate the clearance process of removing lactate and induce a short race-type effort. The inclusion of a couple of short, intense efforts the day before a race is useful in eliminating race-day sluggishness. Keep the efforts short—three to five minutes—and intense, but under no circumstance fatigue yourself.

Morning Heart Rate: Your Wake-up Call

The monitoring of resting heart rate is a valuable tool in gauging the recovery process and establishing individual recovery patterns. I recommend athletes keep a heart-rate monitor next to the bed so that they can quickly strap it on in the morning to check their heart rate and record it before getting out of bed. This record keeping over a long period of time can help indicate heart-rate trends that can be matched to a pattern of individual recovery. Look for lower and higher morning heart rates that correspond to a greater perceived effort in races or workouts. After a few months of data gathering, you should see trends that can help you establish your individual recovery pattern.

Power Naps—There's No Substitute for Sleep

Sleep is an integral part of a body's natural daily recovery cycle. Encourage this by trying to build in an afternoon nap as part of your daily regimen. Nightly sleep should range between 8 and 10 hours. If you are dropping below 8 hours, you could be depriving your body of its ability to recover naturally.

ABOUT THE AUTHORS

CHRIS CARMICHAEL is the founder and chairman of Carmichael Training Systems (CTS). Chris formed CTS in 1999 after spending more than two decades in the sport of cycling. CTS provides personal coaching, creates and manages training programs and camps, and certifies performance-related training products.

Chris coaches cancer survivor Lance Armstrong (winner of the 1999, 2000, and 2001 Tours de France), three-time Olympian George Hincapie, former world champion Dede Demet-Barry, 2000 Olympian Dylan Casey, and 2000 ParaOlympian Ron Willliams. In January 2001, Chris agreed to serve as fitness coach of professional racing's Eliseo Salazar, who finished third in the 2000 Indianapolis 500.

Chris's unique "Train Right"™ methods have been featured on NBC "Nightly News," the Discovery Channel, CBS's "60 Minutes," and ABC's "World News Tonight." In 1999, Chris was awarded the U.S. Olympic Committee's Coach of the Year Award. In 1997, he joined the Union Cycliste Internationale, the international governing body for cycling headquartered in Lausanne, Switzerland, as the Olympic solidarity coaching instructor.

From 1990 to 1997, Chris worked for USA Cycling in Colorado Springs, Colorado, as the national coaching director. He served as head coach for the 1992 and 1996 Olympic teams and coached several world championships teams. Athletes under his direction have won 33 Olympic, world championships, and Pan-American games medals. In 1996, Chris directed "Project '96," USA Cycling's state-of-the-art technology project. During his tenure at USA Cycling, he created the coaching education program, a certification program designed to educate and develop cycling coaches.

A member of the 1984 U.S. Olympic Cycling Team, Chris was part of the first American team to ride in the Tour de France in 1986. Additionally, he was a member of the U.S. National Cycling Team from 1978–1984.

Chris serves on the Coaches Advisory Committee for the Positive Coaching Alliance. He also serves on the USOC/USA Cycling Elite Athlete Task Force.

Chris is co-author of both *The Lance Armstrong Training Plan* (with Lance Armstrong) and *Fitness Cycling* (with Dr. Edmund Burke). His columns and articles have appeared in *VeloNews*, *Bicycling Magazine*, *Inside Triathlon*, and many newspapers.

Chris lives in Colorado Springs, Colorado, with his wife, Paige, and daughter, Anna.

DYLAN CASEY successfully made the transition from an elite national-caliber cyclist in the United States to a top international competitor in 1999. A talented time trialist, Dylan has competed well in individual events against the clock at the Pan-American games, 2000 Olympic games, and the Tour of Spain. He is one of the only U.S. cyclists to win national championships on both the road and the track, winning the U.S. National Time Trial and Individual Pursuit Championships. Racing for the U.S. Postal Service Professional Cycling Team in Europe, Dylan won time trial stages in the Four Days of Dunkerque and the Tour of Luxembourg. Chris Carmichael has been Dylan's coach since 1998.

TIM CROWLEY has been coaching and assisting triathletes, runners, and duathletes for the past 12 years. He holds a pro/elite triathlon license as a competitor. Tim is a certified triathlon and weightlifting coach, as well as a certified strength and conditioning specialist. Tim brings 14 years of multisport racing experience to CTS, ranging from sprint to Ironman distance and from winter triathlon to off-road triathlon and duathlon. Tim has a degree in sports medicine from Springfield College and is based in Marlboro, Massachusetts.

DEDE DEMET-BARRY was one of the most talented and respected American cyclists in the 1990s. Her talents ranged from individual and team time trials to criteriums and World Cup events. Among the dozens of national and international achievements during her racing career are the four U.S. national championship and two world championships medals she won. She finished her career with the Saturn Cycling Team in 2000 and returned to college.

KRISTEN DIEFFENBACH is a third-year Ph.D. candidate in exercise and sport science and sport psychology at the University of North Carolina at Greensboro. She received her M.S. in physical education with an emphasis in sport psychology from the University of Idaho and her B.A. in biology from Boston University. Kristen's areas of concentration include performance enhancement, talent development and overtraining, staleness, burnout, and recovery. Along with coaching cyclists, Kristen is also a certified U.S. Track and Field (USATF) coach with a Level II specialization in endurance training and distance coaching. Kristen competed in cycling, cross-country, and track and field for Boston University. She currently competes in both road and mountain bike events, with an emphasis on endurance and ultra-endurance endeavors.

CRAIG GRIFFIN is a native of New Zealand and began cycling at the age of 11 when his interest in the sport was piqued by his father and grandfather, who were road racers. His father was also the national coach for New Zealand in 1983. Craig was a New Zealand National Team member from 1979–88 and earned five national championship titles, including the 1985 national road title. He was also a member of junior and senior world championship teams.

Craig served as the USAC national endurance track coach for eleven years and worked as a member of the 1992, 1996, and 2000 Olympic coaching staff. He guided Erin Hartwell to the first U.S. Olympic medal in the kilometer time trial, coached the U.S. pursuit team to its first-ever medal in international competition and Mike McCarthy to the first World Individual Pursuit Championship won by a U.S. rider. Athletes working with Craig have won 48 Olympic, World, Pan-American, and World Cup medals and more than 40 elite national titles. Craig was honored as the 1998 U.S. Olympic Committee Coach of the Year for cycling.

GEORGE HINCAPIE has been working with Chris Carmichael since his days on the U.S. Junior National Team. George quickly developed into an elite amateur cyclist in the United States and was a member of the 1992 Olympic Cycling Team. He has raced professionally for the Motorola and U.S. Postal Service Cycling Teams since winning the U.S. Professional Road National Championships in 1998, and he has participated in the Tour de France six times between 1996 and 2001. In 2001, George scored the biggest victory of his career to date by winning Ghent-Wevelgem. He has been an integral part of Lance Armstrong's three Tour de France victories.

RICHARD KATTOUF is a doctor of optometry in Cortland, Ohio, and has been a CTS member since 2000. He is one of the top duathletes in the United States and has competed at the duathlon world championships twice. During the first year he worked with CTS, Rick's national ranking climbed from 30th to 2nd in the 25–29 age group.

MATT KELLY became the first American cyclist to win a cyclo-cross world championship when he won the junior event in Poprad, Slovakia, in 1999. He was the USA Cycling Junior Male Mountain Bike and Cyclo-cross Athlete of the Year in 1999. In his first year as a senior competitor, Matt was a member of the Trek/Volkswagen Professional Mountain Bike Team.

JIM LEHMAN brings a wealth of knowledge to CTS by way of education and experience. He holds a bachelor's degree in psychology and a master's degree in exercise physiology. It was this experience that landed him a position as a resident cycling coach at the Olympic Training Center in Colorado Springs. Jim is a Category 2 on the road and an expert on the dirt. He has worked many USA Cycling regional training camps and has developed numerous programs for national-level athletes. Jim is based in Colorado Springs and is the director of coaching as well as a cycling coach.

ERIK MOEN, PT, CSCS, is a graduate of Pacific Lutheran University and the University of Washington Physical Therapy program. He is the clinic director of an outpatient orthopedic and sports physical therapy clinic in Seattle, Washington. He holds memberships with the American Physical Therapy Association, National Strength and Conditioning Association (Certified Strength and Conditioning Specialist), and USA Cycling–United States Cycling Federation. Erik achieved the elite level of coach with the USCF in 1997 and was given the 1996 Region 5 Expert Coach of the Year Award. Erik works with several Seattle clubs and athletes. These athletes cover all proficiencies and disciplines, including masters world champions in mountain biking and velodrome. Erik lectures nationally on bicycling biomechanics, injury interventions and prevention, retro-fit of bicycle to athlete, and exercise programming.

MIKE NIEDERPRUEM has been involved in cycling as both an athlete and a coach since his college days when he participated in the historic Little 500 at Indiana University. Mike has a bachelor's degree in sport science and a master's degree in exercise physiology, as well as the distinction of being a certified strength and conditioning specialist (CSCS) through the NSCA.

Additionally, Mike has extensive experience coaching both male and female cyclists at the highest level in all disciplines (mountain biking, road, and track). During his tenure at USA Cycling as the manager of coaching education from 1994 until

1998, Mike trained hundreds of coaches as well as athletes. He was the U.S. Cycling team coach at the 1994 Goodwill Games in St. Petersburg, Russia, and the 1996 Pan-American Cycling Championships in Cali, Colombia. Most recently, Mike was the national coaching director for the British Cycling Federation in 1998, where he created the coaching education and development plans for all of the United Kingdom.

PETER REID has been a dominant force in triathlon since his victory in the 1998 Ironman World Championship race in Kona, Hawaii. During his triathlon career, Peter has won seven Ironman competitions. He worked with Chris Carmichael during the 2000 season in preparation for his second Ironman World Championship victory. Both *Triathlete Magazine* and *Triathlon Canada* named Peter as their 2000 Male Long Course Triathlete of the Year.

JIM RUTBERG has been a part of CTS since it began. Originally, as an athlete personally coached by Chris Carmichael, he learned the theory and practice of CTS firsthand. A cum laude graduate of Wake Forest University, he earned a B.S. degree in health and exercise science. In addition to working as a coach, Jim's role at CTS has expanded into software development, content management, and business development. He has competed as a racing cyclist at the elite national level throughout the United States. In 1999, he competed internationally at the Tour de Okinawa as a member of the U.S. National Cycling Team. His years of racing and traveling have taught Jim to apply sound training principles and good nutritional decision-making to busy lifestyles.

SCOTT SCHNITZSPAHN has worked with cyclists, runners, and swimmers as well as athletes who combine those disciplines. Scott is currently a licensed coach in triathlon, cycling, and track and field. He is a USA Triathlon regional coaching director and is competitive as a triathlete, duathlete, and runner. Scott holds a degree in exercise physiology and has great amounts of experience in physiological testing and all aspects of heart-rate training. Scott is based in Roselle, Illinois.

JESS SWIGGERS began his mountain bike career as a downhiller but switched to racing cross-country in 1997. In 1998 he was the Junior National Mountain Bike Champion, and by 1999 the young man from Ramona, California, was the U.S. U23 National Champion. Recognized as one of the promising young talents in U.S. cycling, Jess was invited to be a resident-athlete at the Olympic Training Center in Colorado Springs, Colorado, in 1999 and 2000.

Conrad Stoltz, CTS member and 2000 Olympic team member.

INDEX

Acceleration, 71, 82, 96, 98, 104, 119, 132, 136
  hill, 37
  sprinting and, 94, 97
Adaptation, 8, 161
Aerobic conditioning, 72, 104, 113, 118, 142–43, 146
  building, 25, 32, 51, 52, 98, 119, 137
  cadence and, 77
  maintaining, 42–43, 117
  pedal strokes and, 78
  sprinting and, 96, 98
Aerodynamics, 75–76, 79
Agility, building, 26
Amstel Gold Race, Armstrong and, 41, 42, 52, 129, 130
Anaerobic power, 26, 113, 115, 118
Antioxidants, free radicals and, 175, 181
Armstrong, Lance
  base mileage for, 120
  cadence of, 72, 74, 77
  field tests for, 130
  goals of, 9, 12, 23, 41, 129
  illness/crashes for, 129
  lactate threshold of, 178
  mental barriers for, 21
  recovery by, 182
  sprinting by, 98
  super-compensation and, 36
  tempo workouts and, 119
  training by, 18, 21, 37, 39, 49, 50, 178
  visualization by, 14
Assessments, making, 10, 17, 18, 31, 84
Asymmetries, 159
Athlete-development model, 40
Athletes, 1
  coaches and, 24, 48
Attacking, 25–27, 82–83, 139

Balance, 170
Base miles, 117, 118, 120, 155
bcaa. *See* Branched-chain amino acids
Behavioral patterns, identifying, 20
Benchmarks, finding, 20
Big gears, pushing, 77
Bike-fit irregularities, 160
  injuries from, 158
Bike-handling skills, refining, 42
Bike setup, 75–76
Biomechanics, 160, 161
Blackburn Roadie, 142

Body
  asymmetries, 160
  mind and, 17, 167, 170
  position, 14, 67
  reading, 153
  weight, 20
Braking, downhill, 87, 88
Branched-chain amino acids (bcaa), 175, 181
Breakaways, 41, 81–82, 139, 154
  chasing down, 83, 146
  in criteriums, 89
  energy for, 82
  forcing, 93
  preparing for, 42
  sprinting and, 149
Bridging, 83, 90, 146
British Cycling Federation, on coaches, 24
Bruyneel, Johan, xi, 49, ,139
Buffering capacity, 113
Bumping, 150
Burke, Edmund
  on bcaa, 181
  on carbohydrates/proteins, 174
  Lasik for, 127–28
  on recovery, 179
  on tempo training, 118
Burnout, 167–70

Cable rows, single-leg, 108
Cadence, 14, 73, 74, 110, 122, 138, 160
  aerobic system and, 77
  elevated, 72, 115
  ideal, 132, 159
  increasing, 52, 71, 72, 77
  low, 72, 15
  maintaining, 13, 51, 115
  PI, 143
  sprinting and, 147, 148
  SS, 143
  See also Pedaling
Carbohydrates
  consuming, 175, 179
  proteins and, 174, 180
Cardiac drift, 114
Carmichael, Chris, x, xi, xii, 33, 138, 153, 169
  on recovery, 155
  success and, 55
  training and, 101, 102
  on weight workouts, 146

Carmichael, Chris (continued)
    working with, 31
Carmichael Training Systems (CTS), 31, 101–2, 111
    creation of, xi–xii, 2
    Field Test, 52, 53
    resistance program by, 50
    training at, 50
    training journal software by, 18
Cellular metabolism, 164
Cipollini, Mario, 55, 149
Climbing, 17, 18, 19, 37, 87, 89, 117, 122–23, 130,
        131, 132, 153,154
    cadence for, 52
    heart rate and, 124
    increasing, 53
    learning, 21
    strength and, 104
Coaches
    attitude/demeanor of, 47
    communicating with, 31, 35, 37, 38, 123–24
    goal of, 43
    importance of, 2–3, 7, 30–31, 45
    preparation by, 39, 45
    role of, 24, 48
    styles/philosophies of, ix, 1
Coaching, x, 2, 7–8
    importance of, ix, xii
    strength and conditioning, 106
    teaching and, 8
    training and, 7
Commitment, 9
    mid-term goals and, 13
Communication, coach-athlete, 31, 35, 37, 38,
        123–24
Competition
    training and, ix, 39
    See also Opponents
CompuTrainers, 77
Concentration skills, 56, 57, 59
Conditioning
    physical, 43, 55
    sprinting, 96
    See also Aerobic conditioning
Confidence, 43, 47
    building, 2, 8, 21, 25, 27, 31, 40–42, 48
    sprinting and, 149
    undermining, 57
Contact lenses, 125, 126, 127
    alternatives for, 128
Cooldowns, 110, 114, 116, 132
Coordination, building, 26, 122
Crashes, 42, 87, 88, 129, 135, 148
Crawford, Allan, 120
    tempo workout schedule of, 123 (table)
Criteriums
    preparation for, 89, 90
    tactics for, 89–91
Cross training, 146
CTS. See Carmichael Training Systems
Cue words, 56, 58

Dehydration, 19, 165, 174
    chronic, 142
    limiting, 173
    sodium and, 164
    See also Hydration
Dejonckheere, Noel: on sprinting, 95, 98

Denton, Laurie, xii
Denton, Lila, xii
Denton, Morris, xi–xii
DescendingIntervals (DI), 115, 116, 137
    maximal effort and, 136
Descending skills, 124
    developing, 13, 85–88
    sprinting and, 95
Desire, 9, 12
    mid-term goals and, 13
    success and, 10–11
Details, 14, 48
DI. See DescendingIntervals
Diet. See Eating
Downhill. See Descending skills
Drafting
    effective, 79–84
    time gain/energy savings and, 82
    wind and, 80, 81
Dress rehearsals, value of, 46
Dyson, George, 24

Eating, 33, 168
    while traveling, 141
    See also Meals; Nutrition
Echelons, 80–81
Efficiency, 75, 76–77, 119
Electrolytes, 165, 171
    restoring, 174, 179–80
    water and, 174
Emotional development, 1
Endorphins, 169
Endurance, 26, 55, 75, 89, 177
    building, 77–78, 179
    criteriums and, 91
    goals for, 27
    maintaining, 36, 117
    muscle, 108
    pedaling and, 159
    sprinting and, 96, 98
Energy, 25, 27, 150
    conserving, 52, 84, 148, 149
    focused, 41
    producing, 36
    running output of, 69
    systems, 40, 52
    training and, 43
    wasting, 76
Energy drinks, 173
Exercises
    large muscle mass, 110
    primary, 107
    warming-up, 107
Explosive lifts, 105, 106

FastPedal, 73
Fast-twitch muscle fibers, 104, 118
Fatigue, 164, 167, 172, 182
    cadence/pedal stroke and, 71
    dealing with, 56
    overload and, 36
    recovery and, 119
    running, 70
    signs of, 168
    sleep problems and, 20
Fatty acids, 118, 119, 172
Field sprinting, 89, 145–50

Field tests, 38, 52, 131, 132
    heart rate and, 133
    recording, 133
    repeatability and, 130
Finish area, studying, 46
Fitness, 1, 43, 138, 169
Fixed-gear riding, 23, 74
Flexibility, 159, 160
Fluids
    consuming, 19, 165, 171, 173, 174, 179, 180
    See also Hydration; Sports drinks; Water
Focus, 40, 41
    enhancing, 57, 58
    loss of, 168
    maintaining, 30, 57, 136, 167–70
    problems with, 172
Form, improving, 67
Foundation work, 50, 155
Free radicals, 174–75, 180, 181
Frischkorn, Will, 153
Functional strength training (FST), 104
    principles of, 103, 106–7
    triathlon-specific, 107–8

Gastric emptying, 174
Glasses
    all-weather lenses for, 128
    wearing, 125, 126
Glucose, 118, 173, 175
Glutamine, 181
Gluteus medius, role of, 159
Glycogen, 36, 172
    depletion of, 173
    insulin and, 174, 180
    muscle proteins and, 175
    replenishing, 175, 179, 180
    storage capacity of, 118
Goals, 2, 23
    achieving, 3, 7, 8, 15, 30, 31, 33, 41
    attainable, 12
    coaching, 7, 43
    dream, 12
    evaluating, 9, 12, 14
    fitness, 19
    long-term, 22, 33
    medium-range, 30
    micro, 13, 14, 30
    mid-term, 13, 22
    overload and, 27
    physical training and, 25
    seasonal, 30
    setting, 25, 30
    short-term, 30, 33
    training, 2, 40, 135
    working toward, 32, 43
Gould, Dan, 56
Gravity, running and, 70

Hamstrings
    tendinitis in, 161
    weakness in, 159
Headwinds, sprinting and, 148, 150
Heart rate, 120, 158, 160
    average, 132
    cardiac drift and, 114
    climbing and, 124
    drop in, 173

field tests and, 133
    increasing, 122
    intensity of, 19, 115, 130, 132–33
    intervals and, 30, 116
    lactate threshold, 121, 131
    maintaining, 13, 21, 116
    maximum, 26, 121, 143
    monitoring, 18, 32, 172, 182–83
    nonstable, 121
    pedal cadence and, 73
    PI, 143
    recovery and, 182, 183
    resting, 20, 172, 182–83
    spinning and, 144
    tempo training and, 118, 121, 124
    time trials and, 143
    values, 132, 133
Heart rate monitors, 1, 114, 116, 182
Hewlett-Packard International Women's Challenge,
    167, 168
High-volume phase, 111
HillClimbing, 57
Hincapie, George, x, 136, 143
    coaches and, 101
    goals of, 23, 27
    mental suitcase of, 138
    sprinting by, 95
    tactics of, 26
    tempo workout schedule of, 123 (table)
    training by, 25, 26, 27, 102, 135, 137
    VO_2 max/lactate threshold test for, 120
Holistic approach, 10
Hoyt, Jim, ix–x
Hydration, 131, 142, 163–66
    sports drinks and, 180
    See also Dehydration; Fluids; Water
Hyponatremia, 163, 164, 165

Impact time, shortening, 69
Indoor trainers, 143
Indurain, Miguel, xii
Injuries, 68, 73, 146
    avoiding, 31–32, 157–61
    treating, 157–61
Inside Triathlon, articles from, 3
Insulin, 173
    carbohydrates/proteins and, 174
    glycogen and, 174, 180
Intensity, 118, 143, 158
    calculating, 120
    excessive, 35
    increasing, 117
    maintaining, 40, 143
    sprint, 97
    tempo, 119, 120, 121, 122
    threshold, 120, 129, 132, 133
    training, 73, 120, 131
Internal dialogue, 57
International Olympic Academy, on coaches, 24
Intervals, 13, 35, 117, 160, 171
    Descending, 115, 116, 136, 137
    gears for, 115
    heart rate and, 30, 116
    high-intensity, 36
    MuscleTension, 111
    Power, 137, 142, 143–44
    recovery and, 137, 138, 144

Intervals *(continued)*
 SteadyState, 137, 142–43
 Stomp, 111
 Tempo, 137
Ironman, preparing for, 77

Julich, Bobby, x

Karvonen method, 120
Kelly, Matt, 23
 training by, 113, 116
Kemp, John, 29
Kurreck, Karen, 123

Lactate threshold, 120, 121, 131, 132, 153, 178
 increasing, 133, 142–43
 intensity and, 129
 power at, 137
 training at, 119
Lactate tolerance, 113, 115
Lactic acid, 25, 118
 resistance and, 132
Laser vision correction (Lasik), 125, 126, 127–28
Lateral movement, 70
Learning, opportunities for, 8, 30
Leg-length differences, 160
Leg presses, 146
Leg speed, 93, 122
Liège-Bastogne-Liège World Cup, Armstrong and, 178, 182
Limitations, 11, 21, 22, 33
Lindgren, Laura
 tempo workout schedule of, 123 (table)
 training by, 120
Logistics, racing, 29
Lopez, Manny: goals of, 23

MacCurdy, Chris, ix
Magnetic-load trainers, 114
Mashing, 71, 72, 77, 154, 158–59
Massages, 169, 176
Maximal effort, 115, 136
 recovery and, 137
 sustaining, 129
 variance in, 21
Meals
 pre-race, 47
 while traveling, 141, 144
 See also Eating; Nutrition
Medicine balls, 105, 107
Mental barriers, 56
 overcoming, 21–22
 performance and, 18
Mental breaks, 32
Mental process, 14, 21, 55
 importance of, 9
 mid-term goals and, 13
 training and, 10, 15, 55
Mental skills, 59, 167–68
 building, 15, 43, 56, 57, 77
 physical skills and, 56, 78
Merckx, Eddy, xii
Mercury Cycling Team, 153
Metabolic fuels, 118
Micromanagement, avoiding, 48
Mid-term breaks, 167–70
Mind, body and, 17, 167, 170

Mind-set, 10, 57
Mistakes, learning from, 30, 86
Moninger, Scott, 85, 154
Monovision, 127, 128
Motion compensation, 159
Motion-control problems, 68
Motivation, 11, 31, 58
Motorola Cycling Team, x, 49, 95
Motorpacing, 90
Mountain-bike racing, 32, 35
MT. *See* MuscleTension intervals
Muldoon, Andy: goals of, 23
Muscle groups, weakness/imbalance of, 159
Muscle proteins, 175, 179, 181
Muscle soreness, 172, 175, 182
 sleep problems and, 20
Muscle stress, reducing, 179, 180–81
MuscleTension intervals (MT), 111
Musculoskeletal anomalies, 158, 159, 160, 161
Museeuw, Johan, 139

Naps, 172, 183
National Team Program, x
Neel, Mike: on nervousness, 47
Negative thoughts, countering, 56, 57, 58
Nervousness, avoiding, 47–48
Nutrition, 160
 attending to, 37, 178
 See also Meals; Eating

Ochowicz, Jim, x, xi, 11, 49
Off-season, 23
 training in, 109–12, 113–16, 117–24
OL. *See* One-legged pedaling
Olympic games, 47
 Armstrong and, x, 23, 46
 training for, 45, 63, 102, 103
Olympic lifts, 105, 106
Olympic Training Center, 72
100 percent readiness, 25, 27, 40, 43
One-legged pedaling (OL), 111, 160
Opponents, knowing, 145, 146, 148
Optimal Muscle Recovery (Burke), 174, 179
Orlick, Terry, 56
Orthokeratology (Ortho-K), 125, 126, 127, 128
Overload, 27, 36, 110
Over-speed techniques, 97
Overtraining, 31
 burnout and, 168
 rest and, 170
 signs of, 119, 172
Overwork, 38
 injuries from, 157–61
Oxidative stress
 free radicals and, 174–75
 reducing, 179, 180–81

Pacelines, 80, 81
Pain, 56
 bicycling-related, 157, 158
Pain relievers, caution about, 165–66
Paris-Roubaix
 challenges of, 25–26, 135–36
 Hincapie and, 23, 25–27, 135, 136, 138–39
Partington, John, 56
Pavé sections, negotiating, 135, 138–39
Peaking, 23, 25, 32

Pedaling, 51, 154
  downhill, 74
  fast, 72, 96, 160
  gluteus medius and, 159
  higher cadence, 72
  injuries from, 73, 158
  low-intensity, 173
  lower cadence, 71
  one-leg, 73, 111, 160
  quad bias, 158
  sprinting and, 97
  See also Cadence
Pedaling mechanics, developing, 23, 50, 72–73, 160
Pedal speed, 73, 122
  increasing, 21
  maintaining, 97
  recovery and, 182
Pedal strokes, 77
  aerobic system and, 78
  fluid, 76
  improving, 73–74
  pulling through, 73
  sprinting and, 147
  triathlete, 71
  upper-body movement and, 76
Pelotons, 136, 154, 168
  breakaways and, 82, 83
  riding in, 118
Pelvic dysfunction, 160
Performance, 11, 24, 55, 72, 129
  evaluating, 3, 15, 21, 22
  improving, 7, 8, 58
  injuries and, 157, 161
  mental barriers and, 18
  peak, 23, 25, 50, 179
  recovery and, 176, 179
  training and, 20, 65, 103
  water/sodium intake and, 166
Periodization plan, setting up, 49–50
Personal-positives, 56, 58, 59
Physical skills
  mental skills and, 56, 59
  mid-term goals and, 13
Physical training
  goals and, 25
  mental training and, 78
Physiological errors, injuries from, 158
Physiological markers, 160
Physiological testing, 18, 120
PI. *See* PowerIntervals
Planning, 14, 65, 178, 183
Position
  criteriums and, 89
  fighting for, 136, 149, 150
  sprinting and, 145
Positive counterstatements, 58, 59
Postal Service Cycling Team, 11, 26
  Armstrong and, xi, 49
Potential, 1, 9
Power, 104, 132, 135, 136, 154
  aerobic, 26
  anaerobic, 26, 113, 115, 118
  building, 105, 109, 111, 112
  cadence and, 72
  goals for, 27
  peak, 95, 98, 119, 146
  retaining, 36

  sprinting and, 96, 98
  strength and, 105
  sustainable, 51, 52, 53
  threshold, 131, 137
  training for, 105, 108
PowerIntervals (PI), 137, 142, 143–44
Power meters, 1, 19, 64, 95, 130, 132
Power outputs, 52, 118, 119, 177
PowerStarts (PS), 111, 146, 148
Power words, 59
Preparation, 38, 39, 49, 50, 52, 63, 135
  haphazard, 46–47
  mid-term goals and, 13
  process of, 35
  sprinting and, 145–46
  thoughts on, 45–46
Priorities, setting, 29–30
Programs
  creating, 1, 2, 11, 23, 25–27, 121–22
  feedback on, 24
  maintenance, 142
  resistance, 50
  strength, 104, 107
  See also Training
Progress, 3, 19, 138
Proteins
  carbohydrates and, 174, 180
  consuming, 179
  muscle, 175, 179, 181
PS. *See* PowerStarts
Psychological development, 1

Quickness, 94, 95, 96

R4 System, 179
Race bibles, 145
Range of motion, shortening, 69
Reaction time, sprinting and, 97
Recovery, 50, 132, 169
  before/during exercise, 172–73
  fatigue and, 119
  heart rate and, 183
  indoor, 115, 116
  intervals and, 137, 138, 144
  introduction to, 153–55
  long-term, 172, 175–76
  maximal efforts and, 137
  muscle, 171, 179
  performance and, 176, 179
  planning/establishing, 176, 178, 183
  post-exercise, 172, 173–75
  sleep and, 172, 183
  sprinting and, 95, 96, 98, 147, 148
  stimulating, 138, 181, 182
  strength training and, 110, 111
  time for, 178, 179
  training and, 121, 171–76, 177, 182
  See also Rest
Recovery drinks, 116
Rehabilitation plans, 160
Relaxation, 38, 169
Repeatability, 114, 115, 130
Reps, 108, 111
Resistance
  increasing, 111
  lactic acid and, 132
  pedal, 122

Resistance training, 23, 51, 109–12
    effective, 110, 111
    off-season, 111, 112
    weight lifting and, 109
Rest, 36, 38, 168
    burnout and, 169
    indoor, 116
    overtraining and, 170
    training and, 178
    See also Recovery
Road racing, 32
    criteriums and, 90
Rodriguez, Freddy, x
Roll, Bob, xi
Routines, developing, 46–47
Rules, making, 11, 12
Running, 32
    bike training and, 75
    competition/recreation, 67
    improving, 75
    injuries from, 68
    mechanics of, 67–70
    natural, 67
    tactical decisions about, 84
Rutberg, Jim, xii

Saddle height, 76, 160
Salt tablets, caution about, 165
Self-criticism, support and, 48
Self-image, 17, 18, 22
Self-talk, positive, 58
Serious Cycling (Burke), 118
Sets, 108, 111
Shoes, 68, 142, 160
SI. *See* StompIntervals
Skills, building, 9, 25, 40, 56–57
Sleep, 168
    disrupted, 172
    habits, 19–20, 33
    recovery and, 172, 183
    while traveling, 141
    See also Naps
Slipstream, 80
    See also Drafting
Slow-twitch muscle fibers, 118
Sodium
    consuming, 164, 165
    performance and, 166
    water and, 163–66
Specialization periods, 39, 40, 50
    100 percent readiness and, 43
    race schedule during, 41
    training during, 42
Speed, 79, 119, 154, 177
    improving, 95, 97–98
    leg, 93, 122
    pack, 149, 150
    pedal, 21, 73
    top-end, 93, 97, 98
Spinners, mashers and, 71
Spinning, 143, 169
    heart rate and, 144
    recovery and, 138, 153, 173
    sprinting and, 148
Spin Scan, 77
Sports drinks, 132, 173, 174

rehydration and, 180
    sodium in, 165
Sprinting, 13, 19, 30, 42, 55, 71, 117, 122, 132
    acceleration and, 94, 97
    criterium, 89, 90
    defining, 93–94
    effective, 93
    field, 145–50
    flat, 147
    high-speed, 147
    improving, 93–98
    makeup of, 94–95
    physical/tactical elements of, 93
    power, 98
    recovery from, 95, 96, 98, 147, 148
    training for, 93, 95–96, 146–48
Squats, 146
    one-legged/two-legged, 106, 107
    overhead, 108
    split, 107
SRM, 19, 130
SS. *See* SteadyState Intervals
Stability balls, 106, 107, 108
Stage races, 11, 51, 52
Stationary bikes, 110, 143
SteadyState Intervals (SS), 137, 142–43
StompIntervals (SI), 111
Stomps, 146, 147
Strategy, 9, 11, 26, 33, 35, 64
Strength, 43, 111, 135, 136, 160
    building, 23, 50, 109, 112, 146, 179
    fast-twitch muscle-fiber, 104
    goals for, 27
    maintaining, 104
    mental, 77, 167–68
    power and, 105
    sprinting and, 96, 104
Strengths, 21, 91
    assessing, 17, 18, 84
Strength training, 146
    in-season, 104
    lifts and, 106
    misconceptions about, 103–4
    recovery during, 111
    tools for, 106–7
    triathletes and, 103–8
    year-round, 104
Stretching, 31–32, 110
Strides, shortening, 70
Strokes, smooth, 71, 76, 77
Success, 33, 55–59
Super-compensation, 36
Surges, sprinting and, 148, 150
Sweating, 163, 164
Swiggers, Jess: goals of, 23

T. *See* Tempo intervals
Tactics, 9, 84, 146
    criterium, 89–91
    improving, 42, 177
    running/bicycling 84
    sprinting, 93
    triathlon, 79
Tapering, 35, 37
Team pursuit racing, 63–65
Technical skills, 33

Technique
  errors, injuries from, 158
  running, 67–70
Technology, 1, 2, 64, 68
Tempo intervals (T), 137
Tempo training, 120, 155
  adapting to, 121
  benefits of, 118–19
  examples of, 123 (table)
  heart rate and, 124
  recovery and, 122
  technical considerations for, 122
Tendinitis, 157, 161
Tension-breakers, 38
Time trials, 17, 131, 132
  criteriums and, 89, 90
  heart rate and, 143
  rehearsing for, 46
  training for, 42
  uphill, 130
Timing schedule, 64
Tour de France, 51
  Armstrong and, 10, 12, 23, 39, 42, 49,
    52, 72, 77
  preparing for, 39, 49, 52, 53
  Zülle and, 148
Track racing, 35, 36
Traction, 86, 87
Training, xii, 9, 19, 64
  challenging, 22
  deficits in, 161
  designing, 1, 22, 41, 57
  effectiveness of, 24
  evaluating, 57, 114, 129
  incorrect, 18
  individualized, 123
  indoor, 113–16, 143
  introduction to, 101–2
  maximizing, 113
  maximum sustainable, 21
  models for, 40
  parts of, 114
  recovery and, 121, 171–76, 177, 182
  while traveling, 141
  See also Functional strength training;
    Programs; Workouts
Training blocks, 121, 122, 123
Training camps, 52
Training cycles, 130
Training journals, 18–19, 32, 68, 172
Training pyramid, 40, 41
Transition phase, 50, 111
Travel, rigors of, 141–44
Travel bikes, 142
Triathletes, 71, 84
  training as, 75, 78, 104
Triathlons
  coaching for, ix
  cycling leg of, 79
  draft-legal, 79
  as one sport, 75
Tune Powertap, 19
Turning, practicing, 86

U23 National Team, xii
Union Cicliste Internationale (UCI), 23
U.S. Men's Endurance Track Team, 63
U.S. National Team, 49
USA Cycling, 63, 64

Valgus moment, 159
VeloNews, articles from, 3
Vertical movement, unnecessary, 70
Videotaping, benefits of, 64, 70
Vision, 125
  clear, 126, 128
  correcting, 127–28
Visualization, 14–15, 30, 33, 52
  downhill, 86–87
VO_2 max test, 43, 120, 129, 142
Vuelta a Espana, Armstrong and, 21, 22, 49, 98

Walsh, Charlie, 37
Warming up, 46, 142
  exercises for, 107
  indoor, 114–15
  routine for, 131
  strength training and, 110
Water
  balance, 164
  before/during race, 165
  consuming, 164
  electrolytes and, 174
  intoxication, 163
  performance and, 166
  restoring, 179–80
  sodium and, 163–66
  See also Fluids; Hydration
Weaknesses, 17, 21, 57, 159
Weather conditions, 45, 177
Weightlifting, 23, 50, 51, 109, 146
  See also Strength training
"Whole body" exercises, 110
Workload capacity, 118
Workouts, ix, 2, 50, 122, 129
  climbing, 87
  fixed-gear, 23
  high-intensity, 146
  indoor, 113, 114, 114, 116
  lactate-threshold, 39, 43
  medium-hard, 101
  modification of, 14, 19
  off-season, 117–24
  power, 111, 146
  recovery and, 172
  resistance, 23
  sprint, 98
  tempo, 39, 117–24, 155
  while traveling, 142, 144
  visualization and, 14
  See also Training
World Championships, 47, 63, 64, 65
  Armstrong and, 36, 98

Zabel, Erik, 149
Zülle, Alex, 148

The Triathlete's Training Bible *by Joe Friel*
Maximize your potential and your precious training time with this comprehensive guide to multisport performance.
Paperback • 8 1/2 x 11 • 368 pp. • **1-884737-48-X** • **P-TRIB** • **$19.95**

The Cyclist's Training Bible *by Joe Friel*
Determine your natural ability, train sensibly, and maximize your potential with this comprehensive guide for the competitive cyclist.
Paperback • 8 1/2 x 11 • 288 pp. • Charts and illustrations • **1-884737-21-8** • **P-BIB** • **$19.95**

The Mountain Biker's Training Bible *by Joe Friel*
Friel presents the same system he's used to coach amateur and professional athletes to success since 1980, teaching you to become your own coach and ensuring that you arrive at the start line ready to rumble.
Paperback • 8 1/2 x 11 • 328 pp. • **1-884737-71-4** • **P-BIM** • **$19.95**

Training Plans for Multisport Athletes *by Gale Bernhardt*
A hands-on reference book that includes dozens of detailed training plans tailored for any level of multisport athlete. Part of the Ultimate Training Series from VeloPress.
Paperback • 6 x 9 • 344 pp. • **1-884737-82-X** • **P-PLAN** • **$16.95**

Complete Guide to Sports Nutrition *by Monique Ryan*
Ryan clearly explains the roles meal planning, food strategies, and weight management play in optimizing athletic performance and meeting goals. Part of the Ultimate Training Series from VeloPress.
Paperback • 6 x 9 • 336 pp. • **1-884737-57-9** • **P-NUT** • **$16.95**

VeloNews Training Diary *edited by Joe Friel*
Contains 52 undated, one-week spreads to record every facet of each day's workout.
Spiral-bound paperback • 6 x 9 • 248 pp. • **1-884737-42-0** • **P-DIN** • **$12.95**

Inside Triathlon Training Diary *edited by Joe Friel*
Combines the best in quantitative and qualitative training notation. Undated, so you can start at any time of the year.
Spiral-bound paperback • 6 x 9 • 248 pp. • **1-884737-41-2** • **P-IDN** • **$12.95**

VELO *press*®

Tel: 800/234-8356
Fax: 303/444-6788
E-mail: velopress@7dogs.com
Web: velopress.com
VeloPress books are also available from your favorite bookstore or bike shop.